BECOMING A
MASTER TEACHER

A Guide to a Successful Career in the Classroom

DENNIS HEALY

About the Author

D ennis Healy is chair of the English Department at Dubuque Senior High School and an adjunct professor at the University of Dubuque, both in Dubuque, Iowa. He received both B.S. and M.A. degrees in English at Iowa State University in Ames, Iowa. He has been a classroom teacher for over thirty-three years, and coached both track and cross country for twenty-eight years. He has won numerous awards for teaching, including the Presidential Scholar's Teacher Recognition Award, the Iowa Governor's Scholar Teacher Recognition Award, the Gold Star Award for Outstanding Teaching, the Stanford Sterling Teacher Recognition Award from Stanford University, and Iowa's Outstanding Mentor Award.

Layout and design by Blue Room Productions (memories2movies@aol.com)

Illustrations by Jack Berg

Phone: 563-583-4767
E-mail: challengemath@aol.com
http://www.challengemath.com

Library of Congress Control Number: 2008929434
ISBN 13: 978-0-9679915-6-6
ISBN 10: 0-9679915-6-0

*T*his book is dedicated to the thousands of students I have taught and coached. They have inspired me at every stage of my career to challenge them and to challenge myself.

I include on the next page a note from a delightful international student I taught for a semester. I am humbled by her words and her sentiments.

Dear Mr. Healy,

"More grows in the garden than the gardener knows he has sown." This is a famous Spanish proverb that I feel, perfectly epitomizes the impression and influence, you, Mr. Healy, have left on me as well as your previous students.

I walked into your class on the 17th January, 2006, not knowing what to expect. I was informed that you were a rather "eccentric" character, much like the ones we read about throughout the semester. Not that you're a sociopathic killer ... Or at least I hope not.

I looked forward to a new semester, and a new class that would be both interesting and entertaining, two concepts that seldom come together in the class environment. I found both these things in your class. I felt at home.

Apart from the endless laughs you provided, the most important thing you did for me was believe in me. The encouragement you gave me has extended beyond the walls of Senior High. Thank you very much.

I wrote an essay on "greatness" and how desperately I'd like to achieve it. You encouraged that in me and for that, I am grateful.

"The job of a good teacher is to teach students the vitality in themselves." Joseph Campbell, a noted writer and professor once spoke these words. (I had to google him to find that out.)

As I conclude, I'd just like to say that you have fulfilled Mr. Campbell's idea of what a good teacher is, and although it may feel difficult sometimes getting through to "Holden" like teenagers, you, Mr. Healy, have gotten through to me.

That one little comment you made to me about my writing being "excellent" meant all the world to me. That one comment has inspired me to apply that excellence in all aspects of my life. I left your class today, on the 5th of May, 2006, feeling inspired.

Thank you,
Aisha Isaak

P.S. You should come to Namibia one day, you'd enjoy it!!

Table of Contents

"My heart is singing for joy this morning. A miracle has happened! The light of understanding has shone upon my little pupil's mind, and behold, all things are changed!"

- Anne Sullivan

"Giving advice—about teaching or any other topic—is easy. Modeling teaching in a way that causes the observer to act in a similar way requires considerably more effort. In Dennis Healy's career as an English teacher, department chairman, and mentoring program coordinator, he has earned the right to give advice to aspiring and young teachers precisely because he has been a good model as a teacher. If one definition of a mentor is 'someone whose hindsight can become your foresight,' then the hindsight on which Dennis reflects in his new book, **Becoming a Master Teacher** shows that he deserves to be considered a mentor. Dennis has truly been a 'teacher leader' in the Dubuque Community School District; his insights are worth examining."

--
John L. Burgart
Superintendent of Schools
Dubuque Community School District
2300 Chaney Road
Dubuque, IA 52001-3095

FOREWORD

This book is neither research based nor data driven. Rather, it is based on over thirty years of teaching in the public schools in Dubuque, Iowa. In all my years of attending inservice presentations by "experts," I acquired little "expertise" in the day-to-day challenges of the classroom, and I did not ever learn about developing a career in teaching.

This book is for both new teachers and experienced teachers. For new teachers, it gives a longitudinal view of the growth of a teacher's career. For experienced teachers, it gives suggestions about how to remain vital and to continue to grow as a professional through the final years in the classroom. But most of all, this book is for the students, who deserve the best we can give them. At the end of the movie "Teachers," teacher Alex Jurel says, "They're not here for us. We're here for them. I think they're worth it." Students are the heart of education, and our hearts and minds must be at their best whether it is our first day in the classroom or our last day.

Two specific instances motivated me to write this book. The first occurred at our school's graduation in 2005. The students selected me to be a speaker, representing the faculty. Preceding me on the dais was our principal, Larry Mitchell. In his introductory remarks, he referred to me as a "master teacher," which I felt was a high compliment. But I also asked myself, "What is a master teacher?" His comments led me to reflect for some time on why he used that descriptor, and what qualities I possessed to earn that praise.

The second inspiration came during a bridge game at the home of some friends. One of the foursome, Ed Zaccaro, is a successful author, publisher, and lecturer on gifted education. I taught two of his children, and my wife and I became friends with him and his wife. After a hand, Ed casually asked me, "Why don't you write a book about teaching?" I said something noncommittal, but reflected on his proposal in the days following. I finally called him and said I would do it. He and his wife, Sara, have been instrumental in helping me craft this book. I owe them a great debt of gratitude. I am also grateful to their daughter, Rachel, for designing and laying out the book.

Aside from the external motivation, I wrote this book because I sense some changes in education that underestimate and undervalue the need for career educators to aspire to master teacher status. On the national level, "No Child Left Behind," with its wildly idealistic notion of universal proficiency ("No Child"), and its suggestion of abandonment ("Left Behind") is, at this writing, a flawed law. One group left behind is teachers; to date the government has not funded the portion of the law which provides financial support for professional development for teachers.

On the state level (Iowa, in my case), focus on student performance on standardized tests, the push for mandated state curriculum ("core curriculum"), and revision of teacher evaluation based on eight teaching standards and forty-two competencies have diverted attention and resources from meaningful professional development. Iowa no longer provides tuition reimbursement for teachers. Administrators, already saddled with more responsibilities than ever, simply do not have time to act as career development advocates; rather, they must focus their evaluations on teacher competency rather than professional enhancement.

Locally in my school district, our Individual Professional Development Plan asks no more from teachers than documenting learning strategies that directly affect student achievement (as if that can be irrefutably asserted). Pursuing advanced degrees, attending workshops, and taking courses on line do not meet the requirements for the IPDP.

Our young teachers and our experienced teachers must be internally motivated if they want to improve their content area knowledge and experience other educational opportunities which contribute heavily to attaining mastery.

I fear that our nation is creating a generation of teachers who will be proficient, but will not aspire to mastery because of neglect on national, state, and local levels. A subtitle for this book could be "No Master Teacher Left Behind."

A note on the illustrations: The two teachers, Andy and Allie, represent teachers who begin their careers by interviewing for jobs, and end them as career educators. Mr. and Ms. Master provide expert commentary on the illustrations, using their experience to praise or caution the behaviors depicted in the illustrations. Hopefully, they humanize the issues the illustrations raise.

I chose primarily second person point of view in this book because I view the book as a conversation between the reader and me. I want the book to be as intimate as possible, a contrast to other, more scholarly, more copiously researched, and more formally written books about teaching. I am not a researcher; I do not view education from afar. I am a practitioner; I am immersed in the day-to-day operations of a school. The case studies come completely from my experiences, my colleagues' experiences, and my students' experiences. Not one of the case studies is hypothetical. This book may not be scholarly, but it is authentic.

Finally, I want to recognize those who inspired me on my journey in education. First, my unofficial mentors, Richard Starr and Dale Ross. In the absence of formal mentors, Richard guided me through the first difficult years of teaching. Dale was my undergraduate and graduate advisor at Iowa State University. He freely gave his time and his advice, and was a role model for the accessibility that is so important in helping students. Second, my children, Nolan and Bronwen. I taught both of them, and both read the manuscript and offered valuable information from their experiences with me. Finally, my wife, Brenna, my ultimate editor not only of this book, but in life as well.

February 3, 2008

> *I see myself as a motivated and motivating educator. I thrive on my students' successes. My career goals – to make every class meaningful, to instill a passion for learning in my students, and to remain dynamic and vital in the classroom – will drive me until the day I retire.*
>
> *- Dennis Healy*

**Four characters play significant roles in this book.
Let me introduce them to you:**

Andy and Allie are the two teachers who dominate the illustrations. They represent career teachers from student teaching through retirement. They provide a visual complement to each chapter's commentary on the growth of a teacher's persona.

Andy   *Allie*

Mr. and Ms. Master provide pithy commentary to the illustrations. Both are master teachers, whose knowledge and experience both illuminate and critique the frustrations, triumphs, and challenges which teachers face in their careers.

Mr. Master   *Ms. Master*

INTRODUCTION

The first thing you must know to become a master teacher:

Teaching is an art,
not a science.

Imagine that you decide to learn how to skydive. You've never been in an airplane and you've never been in a building with more than twenty stories. You contact a skydiving school and in a few days, you receive a book (without illustrations) which provides all the instructions. When you call the school to ask when simulations or lessons begin, the representative tells you that you simply need to read the book, memorize the sequence of events, and you'll be ready for your first jump. Impossible, you say? Probably, because there are simply too many parts of the experience that you must simulate before you can successfully make your first jump.

Similarly, becoming a competent teacher takes far more than course work; in fact, most teachers say that they learned more about teaching during student teaching than they did in all the education courses they took. This is not a knock on education classes; rather, it is a commentary on what an amazingly complex profession teaching is.

If teaching were a science, teacher education majors with the highest grade point averages would be the best teachers. Schools wouldn't even interview prospective teaching candidates; all teachers would be hired on the basis of grade point alone. Teachers with advanced degrees would automatically be deemed superior. But this is simply not the case. While advanced degrees add to teachers' breadth and depth of knowledge, they do not ensure excellence in the classroom. Components such as commitment, passion, compassion, sense of humor, and insight into human behavior are qualities of teaching which cannot be measured on any scale. No matter how much the "experts" try to affix measurable paradigms to education, they will never be able to ascertain who will become the best teachers, and even more importantly, who will make a career of teaching.

Ms. Ann Spired

Mr. Vanced Degree, B.A., M.A., M.A.T.

So, what is the definition of a master teacher? Becoming a master teacher involves much more than academic proficiency. I teach a short story, "Gryphon," by Charles Baxter, in which a wildly imaginative substitute, Miss Ferenczi, takes over a fourth grade class from the staid, predictable, but steady Mr. Hibler. In order to compare those two teachers, I first ask my classes to identify the characteristics of a successful teacher. Invariably, the following traits emerge: flexible, humorous, understanding, consistent, makes learning fun, doesn't play favorites, well organized, doesn't talk down to the students, enjoys young people, enjoys the job. These traits lead to the following definition:

> **A Master teacher combines the pedagogical, interpersonal, organizational and emotional skills necessary to inspire students on all levels to learn and achieve.**

How will you know when you are a master teacher? Success in teaching is very difficult to measure. Most states recognize the accumulation of degrees, credits, and longevity in determining salaries, but few affix "Master Teacher," to a teacher's title. There are some extrinsic rewards which teachers receive, such as teacher of the year or local, state, regional, or national awards. But few of these awards are objectively determined, and some are politically influenced. I have received some of those awards, but to me, recognition by students is the most significant measure of my success. After all, who evaluates teachers most closely and thoroughly? The students, of course! Who actually sees you teach more often than your own students? No one! Students see you on your best days and your worst days. They don't stop in four or five times during the year to evaluate. They evaluate you every day. And make no mistake about it, students are the most discerning critics. So it stands to reason that their acceptance, respect, and praise are the most valid and reliable (to use statistically relevant diction). Recently, I saw a student who had just graduated from a small, highly-regarded private college. As we chatted, she told me that a class she took from me when she was a senior was the best class she took in all her years of schooling. I was touched. Several years ago I received a Presidential Scholars Teacher Recognition Award and an Iowa Governor's Scholars Teacher Recognition Award. Both of those awards came from student nominations.

I cherish those awards more than any I have received in my years of teaching.

So if teaching is more art than science, how does one become an effective and respected teacher? It takes time, effort, hard work, reflection, and a burning desire to improve. The remaining chapters of this book focus on the journey that leads to mastery teaching and the navigational skills you will need to make safe passage.

Chapter 1:

The Student Teaching Experience

The second thing you must know to become a master teacher:

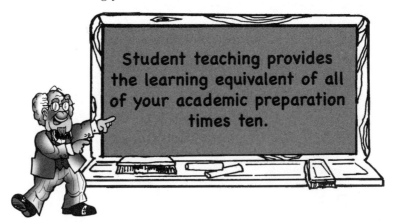

Student teaching provides the learning equivalent of all of your academic preparation times ten.

Student teaching is the most critical component of the academic preparation for becoming a teacher. It comes at the end of the course work, and forms a bridge between course work and actual teaching. It presents a real-world opportunity to experience delivering lessons, to immerse oneself in the school's culture (students, staff, administration), and to decide if teaching is a suitable career.

Students who begin student teaching should be aware that success hinges on the following:

- The cooperating teacher
- The college or university supervisor
- The students you teach
- The principal
- The school culture
- Your own persona

Just as you are evaluated by both your cooperating teacher and your supervising professor, take into account the quality of those who evaluate you.

Note: Before you begin student teaching, visit your assigned school if you can. The school may look daunting, but it's better to experience the waves of nervousness before you walk in on your first day.

THE COOPERATING TEACHER

When I student taught, my cooperating teacher was good-looking and well-dressed. However, I noticed that her grasp of the content areas was not that of a master teacher. During her introduction to a unit on twentieth century American Literature, she informed the class that John Steinbeck, rather than Ernest Hemingway, wrote <u>A Farewell to Arms</u>. Out of respect, I did not correct her on this point (avoid that at all costs), but I sensed that she was not as scholarly as I thought English teachers should be.

It is important to respect your cooperating teacher. A number of years ago, I had a lively and animated student teacher. Students enjoyed his energy and enthusiasm. He was, however, impulsive. One day as he wrote plans on the board for the next class, I sat in my desk explaining the next day's assignment to the class I was teaching. I noticed that the students were not looking at me and chuckling. I turned, and my student teacher was mimicking me behind my back. After school I addressed

"Only those who will risk going too far can possibly find out how far one can go."
                                                                    - T.S. Eliot

him firmly and emphatically, stating that if he ever did that again, I would not allow him back in my classroom. He apologized profusely, but it was hard for me to forget such a disrespectful act. Thankfully, we finished the semester on good terms, and he is currently a career teacher in another state.

I must address one additional issue regarding the pool of available cooperating teachers. Because many colleges and universities provide low compensation for cooperating teachers in comparison to the hours of mentoring the cooperating teachers provide, some teachers refuse to take student teachers. Unfortunately, many of these teachers who feel exploited by the colleges and universities are also some of the finest teachers in their buildings. This combination of low compensation and teacher refusal results in a smaller number of available cooperating teachers. If an outstanding teacher declines to take you as a student teacher it may have nothing to do with you.

Cooperating teachers vary tremendously in experience, personality, and attitudes. In fact, you may encounter any of the following types of cooperating teachers:

The Do It Alls: The harried activity sponsor. These cooperating teachers may accept student teachers because they are too busy outside of the classroom sponsoring co-curricular activities and need someone to reduce their work loads. The advantages to having cooperating teachers like these are that you develop respect for the work load of teachers/activity sponsors and you will have autonomy in the classroom within a relatively short time. The disadvantages are that they will be hard to conference with for any length of time, they are usually in a great hurry, and they may be more interested in co-curricular activities than they are in the classroom and may not be great models for effective teaching.

The Marginals: These cooperating teachers take student teachers because they are not successful or happy in the classroom or they are losing energy or interest in teaching and cannot deal with full-time contact with students. If you happen to be placed with a Mr. Marginal, you may experience the following challenges: first, you may have to resurrect the classes; that is, you may be teaching classes that students either barely tolerate or loathe; second, you will not receive much guidance because Mr. Marginal does not have the spark that successful teachers do; and third, you may mistakenly feel you are not as effective when, in fact, the classes are already irreparably damaged by the classroom environment which Mr. Marginal established long ago. The upside with a Mr. Marginal is that if you spark the students to enjoy learning and look forward to coming to class when you teach, you know you can do well in your first position.

"Others can stop you temporarily - you are the only one who can do it permanently."
                                                                     - Zig Ziglar

The Résumé Builders: These cooperating teachers are not long for the classroom, and taking student teachers provides them with résumé fodder. There is a significant advantage to having these teachers: they are motivated and they are conscientious because they have career ladders to climb. They will be well-organized, punctual and attentive because recommendations from college professors receive extra weight on their portfolios. Their interest in the content areas may not be as strong as that of career teachers because their graduate work centers primarily on administration courses. Mr. Résumé Builders are a mixed bag.

The Magnificents: If you get a Ms. Magnificent for a cooperating teacher, fall on your knees and thank the education gods and goddesses. Ms. Magnificents are not threatened by student teachers. In the hands of Ms. Magnificents, you will be nurtured, tutored, mentored, advised, appreciated, celebrated, and guided with the deftest of hands. Ms. Magnificents enjoy the classroom, the students, the school, and the subject matter and have the talent to communicate all of that to you. The only disadvantages Ms. Magnificents pose are that the classes will behave well regardless of who is teaching them, and you may not be prepared for the testing your own students will give you when you take your first position. If you have inclinations toward teaching, Ms. Magnificents will reinforce them.

"If you find a path with no obstacles, it probably doesn't lead anywhere."   *- unknown*

THE COLLEGE/UNIVERSITY SUPERVISOR

The supervisor from the college or university you attend will play a role in your ultimate placement because he or she will evaluate you and grade your performance. You will have far less contact with the supervisor, but you will probably receive equal or nearly equal credits as you do from your cooperating teacher. The following tips will enhance your relationship with the supervisor:

- Stay in contact, especially if problems arise. If your placement is not working, speak to your cooperating teacher first! Keep the lines of communication as direct as possible. If the problem persists, schedule a meeting with both cooperating teacher and supervisor. At worst, you may receive a new placement; at best, you can resolve the issues and continue.

- E-mail provides an excellent avenue for communication with the supervisor. Don't lose touch! As the student teacher experience continues, be sure that your supervisor stays abreast of your progress so that your final grade from him or her accurately reflects your performance.

- Be sure that your supervisor observes you and compiles the necessary documentation to adequately evaluate you. Be confident that at the end of student teaching you received the closest scrutiny. If you disagree with your grade, insist that the supervisor provide documentation that justifies the grade you receive. Be thankful if your supervisor visits frequently and tracks your progress. It's comforting. One of my colleagues did his student teaching through a state university. His supervisor did not observe him until the last day of his student teaching experience, and did not announce his visit. On that day, with approval of the cooperating teacher, my colleague had a pizza party for his students and played hangman during the period the supervisor observed him. My colleague received a B from his supervisor for student teaching.

The illustrations on the following page show the importance of maintaining frequent communication on such issues as scheduling observations.

"I touch the future. I teach."   **- Christa McAuliffe**

In addition to your evaluators, there are other important individuals and groups that are crucial to your success.

THE STUDENTS YOU TEACH

Nothing can prepare you for the experience of standing in front of a class of twenty-five young people for the first time. I was so nervous the first time I took over a class that I have no recollection of what I said. You quickly learn that there are also twenty-five life stories sitting in front of you. This is humbling, believe me. In any given class of this size, and depending on grade level, you could have students on powerful medications, students high on other drugs, students dealing with their parents' divorces, students who face bullying every day, students who bully other students every day, students who rarely attend school, students who are obsessed with grades, students who are neglected or abused at home, students who are not living at home, students who are pregnant or who have made other students pregnant, students who are depressed, or students who are parenting their parents or their younger siblings.

Dealing with his parents' divorce

Neglected at home

Obsessed with grades

Faces bullying every day

This is an incomplete list, of course. Facing the complexity of these student issues is the single most challenging aspect of engaging all students in learning. That is why it is so important to know your students as quickly as possible. Spend the time you have at the beginning of student teaching when you observe (before you teach) to familiarize yourself with the students' names, and observe the students closely. Talk to your cooperating teacher about the classes you will teach and the students you will teach to prepare yourself for the diversity you will encounter. During this time, communicate with the students-know them and let them know you, and establish appropriate boundaries from the beginning. Focus on your teaching persona; tell your students to call you Mr. or Ms. Even as a student teacher, you are not a buddy; you are a teacher.

THE PRINCIPAL

Introduce yourself to the principal if you were not formally introduced at the time of placement. Schedule a short meeting before you begin actual classroom teaching. This enables you to assert your professional approach to the building's leader, and a good first impression may pique the principal's interest in you as a future candidate for a position. Near the end of your teaching experience, it is also a good idea to request a mock interview with the principal of the school at which you student teach. The past principal at my school conducted mock interviews with all student teachers. He enjoyed the interactions, and the student teachers thanked him for the opportunity. It is excellent practice and can relieve the anxiety of the first real job interview. It also provides you an opportunity to have your portfolio ready for the interview process. A seasoned principal will notice aspects of your interview responses that need sharpening as well as parts of your portfolio that may need strengthening or clarifying.

SCHOOL MISSION STATEMENT
The mission of Dubuque Senior High School is to provide a climate of mutual respect and support where all may develop their intellectual, creative, social and physical potential.

Good interview. Sharpen your knowledge of inclusion issues and shorten some of your responses. You are ready for a job.

"A good teacher is like a candle - it consumes itself to light the way for others."   *- Author unknown*

THE SCHOOL CULTURE

Student teachers are easily overlooked in school settings. They are frequently mistaken for students, and have minimal contact with the rest of the staff. To increase your visibility do the following things: attend school activities such as musical performances, dramatic performances, and sporting events; volunteer to assist with co-curricular activities; observe as many teachers as possible (beyond what your program requires). These efforts will make you visible to more students and allow you to observe a range of teaching styles. You will find that immersing yourself in the school's culture not only makes you more a part of the school, but it also allows students to see your commitment and to gain respect for your efforts. Becoming a part of your school is critical to becoming a respected teacher.

To increase your knowledge of the staff, eat lunch in the faculty lunch area, or if there is not a designated area, eat with a group of teachers. This is a good time to observe what your future colleagues may be like. Over the years I have been disappointed at the amount of negativity in the faculty lounge. I am selective about my lunch companions and I have actually left the lunch area when the conversation became too toxic. I have no interest in negativity. Teachers who spend a great deal of time running down students are generally unhappy and not well-respected by either faculty or students. Avoid these people at all costs. Their bad attitudes contribute nothing to effective teaching.

"A teacher affects eternity. She can never tell where her influence stops."
                                                                — *Henry Brooks Adams*

YOUR OWN PERSONA

If you are a young student teacher (the early twenties is average), it is important to differentiate yourself from your students at all levels. Remember: You are in school to be their teacher, not their friend. Strive to be friendly with students, but avoid acting like or looking like their peer. Establish boundaries in both appearance and demeanor.

Students react strongly to appearances, and any effort on your part to look or act like them will influence them to see you as a peer, not a teacher. Dress conservatively and speak formally to create the necessary space between you and them. Trying to look older doesn't always work. A student at our school asked a student teacher to the prom, even though her appearance was appropriately adult.

I strongly recommend that you have students address you professionally. If students ask if they can call you by your first name, say, "Certainly." If they ask you what it is, reply, "Ms." or "Mr.". Student teaching is hard enough without having to redefine your role with students.

Most important, be sure to control that over which you have the most control: your performance. Being respectful, punctual, conscientious, studious, communicative, and committed to your role as student teacher will have greater influence on your performance than the cooperating teacher and the supervisor. Student teaching represents a major shift in your life, a shift which acquaints you with the daunting tasks which confront teachers every day. By the end of student teaching, you should know if you are willing to make a commitment to the teaching profession. Reflect deeply, and if you decide to teach, get ready for the next step: Interviewing.

I wrote the following poem to a student teacher at the end of his student teaching experience. He is now a very successful teacher in a large urban high school.

"A teacher who is attempting to teach without inspiring the pupil with a desire to learn is hammering on cold steel."   - Horace Mann

TO MICHAEL

The hardest job you'll ever do
Next to raising children
Is being a student teacher.

The room isn't yours (you don't have a key)
The text isn't yours (you didn't select it)
The desk and its clutter aren't yours (you'll keep a tidier desk)
The students aren't yours (you'll assume them for awhile).

Students, the keenest and least forgiving critics, watch from
all corners of the room
The cooperating teacher watches from the back of the room,
knits his brow and fidgets
The supervisor appears occasionally and watches,
then dispenses forms to complete
For observations
For evaluation
For verification
For matriculation
For certification
He looks collegiate,
disjunct from the world you now inhabit.

Your identity is fragmented
Teacher or student?
Professional or professional in embryo?
Friend or apprentice?
Progressing or regressing?
Confident or terrified?

Respected or muttered about?
Buoyed by a smile or crushed by a sneer?
But you persevere
You face the students who aren't really yours
You teach in the desk that doesn't quite fit
You curse when you arrive early and the door is locked
Leaving you outside
With a backpack full of magic
And a soul to share.

The magic will take time
Trials, errors, adding and subtracting
Years of ingredients
Before it works.

Your soul will be tested, bruised and buffeted
Before it can touch the bruised and buffeted
In your class.

So wait by the door
And look in and watch and ask and listen and work
and create and know students (all students)
And care and love and cry and cry out loud and laugh
And laugh
For several years.

One day the magic will come
You will say, "I will send for Dennis to visit my class"
Then you will realize that you don't have to.

Then you will be a teacher.

CASE STUDY #1

CONFISCATING NOTES FROM STUDENTS

You are teaching a large class. The students are working quietly on an assignment. Ever vigilant, you notice a student passing a note to another student.

What do you do?

Note: I handled this incident poorly.

Discussion of this case study on page 187

CASE STUDY #2

MISTREATMENT
OF SUPPORT STAFF

You are a young teacher in your second or third year at your school. One day you are in the main office waiting to meet with the principal to schedule an observation for your evaluation. As you sit in the office, an older, experienced teacher comes into the office and begins a discussion with the receptionist, who also manages the textbooks in the building. You can hear the conversation. The teacher gives the receptionist a list of names of students who have not turned in textbooks and asks her to notify the students within the next hour. The receptionist says that she can't do that right away because she just received a shipment of supplemental texts that she needs to enter into the system and to number individually. The teacher becomes angry, raises his voice and says, "To hell with the new books. I need those textbooks now!" He then storms out of the office muttering something that includes "damn secretaries."

What would you do?

Discussion of this case study on page 188

CASE STUDY #3

DISCIPLINE OUTSIDE THE CLASSROOM

One of the more difficult issues you will face as a young teacher is disciplining students with whom you are not acquainted outside the familiar confines of the classroom.

One afternoon at school as I walked down a nearly empty hallway, I noticed a student at his locker getting ready to leave for the day. He gathered his books and put on his hat. In our building, students are not allowed to wear hats. Ahead of me was another teacher, who spotted the student and called out, "Hey you, take off the hat!" in a stern voice.

The student turned to the teacher and said, "I'm on my way out of the building."

The teacher replied, raising his voice, "I don't care where you are going, take off the hat!"

The student pointed to the front door and said, "I'm leaving the school."

The teacher, now approaching the student, yelled, "Take off the hat, pal!"

The student, finally exasperated, yelled, "I'm leaving!"

The teacher, now in the student's face, screamed so everyone on the floor could hear, "Don't yell at me, son! We're going to the office!"

And off they went.

How would you handle a situation like this?

Discussion of this case study on page 190

CASE STUDY #4

REEFER MADNESS

As you near the end of your student teaching semester, your cooperating teacher invites you and your fiancée to his home for dinner. Your cooperating teacher has been wonderful: understanding, supportive, and helpful. He has a strong rapport with his students because of his knowledge and because he's hip. You admire his ability to relate to his students.

When you and your fiancée arrive for dinner, your cooperating teacher, who prepared most of the meal, offers you a beer, which you accept, then he asks you to join him in the den while his wife puts the finishing touches on the preparation.

When you sit down, the cooperating teacher opens a drawer and takes out a pipe. He asks you if you would like to smoke some marijuana with him to, as he says, "Whet your appetite." Although you know people who smoke occasionally, you do not.

What do you do?

- **Refuse, then report the teacher to the principal?**

- **Refuse, saying that you do not indulge?**

- **Agree, only to be sociable?**

- **Leave with your fiancée immediately to avoid the uncomfortable situation?**

Discussion of this case study on page 193

CASE STUDY #5

INAPPROPRIATE COMMUNICATION IN THE CLASSROOM

You start a class as usual by taking attendance and directing students to begin an assignment. As the students begin to work, a white male student looks at a female African American student across the room and says, in a sarcastic tone, "Hey, _____, what are you doin' after school, hangin' with the other hos and bitches?" The student does not respond, but is embarrassed and withdraws for the rest of the period.

What do you do?

Discussion of this case study on page 195

Chapter 2:

Interviewing

The third thing you must know to become a master teacher:

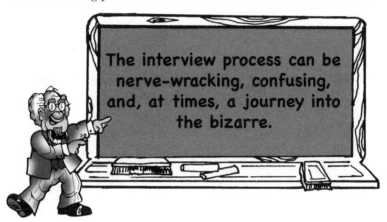

The interview process can be nerve-wracking, confusing, and, at times, a journey into the bizarre.

I spoke recently with a young man who, at the time, had successfully completed his student teaching and was interviewing for jobs. He told me that at one interview the principal asked him, "You look quite young, and you're short. How will students and staff distinguish you from the students?" He thought to himself, "What can I say? Promise that I'll undergo cosmetic surgery to implant wrinkles in my forehead and cheeks? Wear bell bottom houndstooth polyester slacks, elevator shoes, and shirts with oversized collars? Drink pots of coffee and fifths of scotch every day so I can age prematurely?" He was stumped, and stammered through a response which included assertions that he would dress professionally and maintain a serious demeanor. Although you cannot predict the nature or the extent of the questions the interview team will pose, being prepared, poised, and professional will ensure that you have the best chance of making a good impression on your interviewers.

Well-trained administrators and teachers can glean a great deal from interviewees in a short period of time. They will ask challenging questions, and they will observe your body language as they listen to your responses. Your demeanor, tone, and carriage must convey your readiness to assume a teaching position, which means that you must demonstrate that you can control a classroom full of students, and also engage them enough in learning to ensure progress.

I have been a member of numerous interview teams for teachers and administrators, and that experience informs the advice I give in this chapter.

To give a good interview, you must focus on the three phases of the process:

- **Preparing for the interview**
- **The interview itself**
- **Post-interview interactions and developments**

"Good teaching is one-fourth preparation and three-fourths theater."   *- Gail Godwin*

PREPARING FOR THE INTERVIEW

Consider these points as you get ready for the interview:

• When contacted for the interview, take appropriate notes regarding the site and time.

• Look up information about the school so that you are informed about the size, student demographics, and the school's recent achievements.

• Arrive at least a half hour early for the interview and check in immediately in the main office. If the interview team is not ready, take some time to explore the school to get an initial "feel" for the school culture. Positive displays of student awards, cleanliness, and spaciousness can all signal a favorable school environment. Commenting on these features in the interview will impress the interview team.

• Dress professionally, but don't overdress. Present your best, but your real, self. Avoid interviewing in a new suit or dress. Strangely, interviewers may think that you have no other formal clothes, and may think that you look artificial. Rather, wear what you would wear on your most dressed-up day of teaching. In short, look like a teacher! Hint: If you know the school's colors and have appropriate clothing to match, wear it. It shows a symbolic connection with the school.

• Bring something to share with the interviewers. Have a lesson you designed for student teaching, or a paper you wrote for a class, or a project you did which reveals your research skills. Some interviewers will request artifacts, some will not. Be prepared for anything.

• Between the time you meet the principal and others involved in the interview and the time the formal interview begins, be as composed as you can be. Make eye contact, make positive comments about the school, and learn the names of your interviewers as quickly as possible. Pick up nuances in the small talk period that may indicate the person-alities, attitudes, and philosophies of the interview team members.

THE INTERVIEW

Most interviewers must provide documentation from the interview process to jus-tify their appointments. Candidates, especially transfers from within the school system, may request specific reasons why they are passed over. Because of that, interviewers often use rating systems to evaluate the candidates. Don't be sur-prised if the interviewers write a great deal during the interview. Copious note taking does not indicate either excellence or failure; it is part of the information gathering process of the interview. Focus on the following:

• Stay composed physically; don't fidget! Tapping your feet, drumming your fingers on the table, folding and unfolding your hands reveal nervous-ness, and no matter how directly you answer the questions, your body lan-guage will compromise an otherwise strong showing. Above all, do not admit you are nervous!

• Answer all questions directly; Don't ramble! Respond precisely to what each question asks. A good idea is to repeat the question as the opening of your response. Emphasize your strengths and have a plan to address any deficiencies you have regarding your academic preparation and the assignment for which you are interviewing. State your willingness to attend workshops, take classes, or do work on your own to show your desire to do whatever it takes to fill the available position.

• If you forget a question, ask the questioner to repeat it. Failure to adequately respond to a question will cause the interviewers to wonder how strong your listening skills are, and listening is one of the most important skills a teacher possesses.

Allie - the direct answerer

Allie - the befuddled answerer

• Avoid excessive confidence and excessive self-deprecation. Administrators are well aware that prospective new teachers who think they know all the answers are in for a rude awakening on the first day of school. Overconfidence actually reveals a lack of awareness of the challenges of teaching. On the other hand, interviewees who continually downplay their skills lead interview teams to worry about their ability to command a classroom. Be confident, not cocky. Acknowledge areas which you need to strengthen, but don't dwell on them.

"There is no elevator to success. You have to take the stairs."
- Unknown

• Anticipate bizarre questions. Be prepared for the unexpected. Some interviewers like to see how candidates respond to unanticipated questions. You could be asked what you have been reading lately for pleasure, what your favorite color is (check the school's colors for this one), what your favorite song is or what your theme song would be, what bird or flower you'd like to be, where you want to be ten years from now, what three wishes you would make if you could, and other such nonsense. Responses to these questions fall under the creative category, so trust your instincts.

• Review all educational jargon from recent texts and periodicals. Invariably, your interviewers will not be able to restrain themselves from asking questions replete with contemporary educational diction and catch phrases which they banter about in staff meetings. Be prepared to expound on the following:

√ **The school's mission statement**
√ **Paradigm shifts in education in recent years**
√ **District benchmarks and standards**
√ **Vertical and horizontal articulation**
√ **Engaged learning**
√ **Technology proficiency**
√ **Learning strategies**
√ **State and national education initiatives**
√ **Talented and gifted education**
√ **Special education**
√ **Standardized testing**
√ **Differentiation of instruction**

"He who opens a school door, closes a prison."   *- Victor Hugo*

• Stay focused throughout the interview. Although you may have to respond to an extensive list of questions, remain clear and responsive. Interviewers will note your stamina, a crucial component to surviving the first year in the classroom. The interview could last over an hour.

• At the end of the formal questioning period, have your own questions ready. Interviewers will appreciate appropriate questions about the teaching assignment, room location, technology assistance, and availability of curriculum guides.

• Ask for a time line for hiring if the interviewers do not provide it. The hiring game is tricky for both you and the principals. You may receive other offers, the school may interview other candidates, and some candidates turn down job offers. Request prompt notification when the principal makes her or his decision so you can either plan a moving date or redouble your efforts to secure a position at another school.

• Finally, thank the interview team for the opportunity to interview. Thank each interview team member, by name if possible, and project confidence and composure as you leave. Shake hands with everyone on the interview team. Remember, first and last impressions are extremely important. Positive closure could be a factor in your appointment.

"The third-rate mind is only happy when it is thinking with the majority. The second-rate mind is only happy when it is thinking with the minority. The first-rate mind is only happy when it is thinking."
                                                                — *A.A. Milne*

POST INTERVIEW

Once you are away from the interview site, reflect on your performance, focusing on what you felt you did well and what you could improve on. All of us have left discussions feeling we could have said more and responded more intelligently and more thoroughly to questions, but remember, interviewing for a job is a stressful experience. Make a quick list of your strengths and weaknesses, reflect on the questions the interviewers asked, write down what you will do in the next interview to improve your performance. Consider these additional activities:

"*The goal of education is to replace an empty mind with an open mind.*"
                                                    - Malcolm Forbes

• Write a thank you note to the primary interviewer. Make it brief, but appreciative in tone.

• Continue to schedule interviews until you commit to a job. Having another offer may motivate the school you are most interested in to offer you a contract. Remember, nothing is legally binding until you sign a contract!

• If the school notifies you that you did not get the position, consider calling the school to talk to the primary interviewer. You may not have been hired for reasons out of your control. Perhaps the position required a special certification that you do not have. Perhaps the school granted a transfer to someone within the school, but was required by law to post the position and conduct interviews before making the transfer. You may have given the best interview but did not get the job. It's important to know that you did a good job interviewing. In addition to asking why you didn't get the job, ask for an assessment of your interview. A seasoned principal will give you valuable information regarding your interview performance to which you can compare your self-evaluation, thereby increasing your chances of improving your next interview.

• If you receive an offer that does not appeal to you, think carefully before signing a contract. If you desperately need a job, you may have to take a less than ideal position. But in doing so, you risk having a difficult first year, one that may drive you from teaching. A young man who did his observation with me had offers from two small high schools, both of which included six preparations and two head coaching positions. Because he wanted a teaching job in a larger high school, he opted instead to coach and substitute for a year in his home town (Dubuque, Iowa). He resumed interviewing in Dubuque as positions became available. Our school district hired him for a part-time teaching job the next year, and the following year he became a full-time teacher and assistant coach at our school. So, think seriously about teaching load, class size, extra duties, and desirability of the community before undertaking the challenging task of teaching full time.

"Real difficulties can be overcome; it is only the imaginary ones that are unconquerable."
                                                    - Theodore Vail

• When you accept a position and receive a contract, read the contract from beginning to end. Being knowledgeable about contract language– sick leave, health and dental coverage, extra-duty pay, evaluation proce- dures, salary schedule (including longevity and educational attainment)– will make you a more informed teacher, save you money, and will allow you to set additional educational goals.

• Finally, when you sign that first contract, celebrate!

CASE STUDY #6

DEALING WITH SUBSTANCE ABUSE

You supervise a study hall for students who are at risk. Although the study hall is small, you must oversee students' work and academic progress daily. Early into the semester, one of your students displays signs of marijuana use: bloodshot eyes, slow reaction to questions, and the odor of marijuana on his clothes.

Almost daily, he asks to use the restroom. One day when he comes back, the odor of pot is so evident that other students look at each other and smirk. After class, you talk privately to the student, asking directly if he is using marijuana. He denies it.

The next time he asks to use the restroom, you have another teacher cover your class while you check on the student. When you enter the restroom, you smell pot and see the student coming out of a stall still holding a small pipe.

What do you do?

- **Take him immediately to the assistant principal's office for discipline?**

- **Take him immediately to the school nurse and treat his case as a medical problem first?**

- **Confiscate his pipe and call the police from your room?**

- **Tell him that you will refer him to drug counseling, and if he does, you will not report the incident?**

Discussion of this case study on page 197

CASE STUDY #7

PLAGIARISM

You are teaching a class which requires a research paper. Students must meet requirements regarding outlining, note taking, documenting sources, writing a draft, and making corrections on the draft. One of your students lags in all these areas, but when the draft is due, he produces an excellent paper.

As you look the paper over, you notice that while the paper is on a contemporary topic, none of the references is within the last four years. Then you make a scary discovery. You go back into your files of excellent research papers, and notice that the student has copied his sister's research paper, submitted four years ago, word for word!

This is an unambiguous example of plagiarism.

What do you do?

Discussion of this case study on page 199

CASE STUDY #8

STRESS CARRIERS IN THE FACULTY LOUNGE

You are a young teacher, in your third or fourth year. Your career is going well, and students respect you as a skilled and caring teacher. The toughest part of your day, however, is your duty-free lunch period in the faculty lounge. Two teachers dominate the discussions in the lounge, and they are both consistently negative. Their discussions center on a few favorite themes: how ill-prepared students are; how lazy they are; how their parents don't care; how they won't do homework; how little they learned in previous grades; how poorly behaved they are.

You do not enjoy lunch. In fact, you have to refocus before returning to class, where you find little evidence of the traits the teachers harp on in the lounge.

What do you do?

- **Stop going to the lounge for lunch?**

- **Confront the teachers on their negative attitudes?**

Discussion of this case study on page 201

CASE STUDY #9

BREAKING UP FIGHTS

You have just finished lunch in the teacher section of the cafeteria. You have some work to do to prepare for your next class, so you leave a little early. You take your tray to the appropriate area, and as you exit the cafeteria, a fight breaks out between two girls immediately in front of you. The girls are already engaged; one has punched the other and they are now locked in battle.

What do you do?

- **Find an administrator?**

- **Break up the fight yourself?**

- **Tell students to break up the fight while you find an administrator?**

Discussion of this case study on page 203

CASE STUDY #10

CREATING AND MAINTAINING REASONABLE CLASS GUIDELINES

At the beginning of the year, a teacher hands out his class guidelines and policies. In one section, he clearly states that students bring paper and pen and pencil to class daily, and that failure to bring these items will result in zeros on tests or quizzes.

Two weeks into the marking period, the teacher gives a chapter test. One student forgets his pencil and pen. The teacher says, "Sorry, you'll have to take a zero on the test. Maybe this will help you remember the next time."

What is your reaction to this scenario?

- **Good for the teacher! We must teach students to be responsible.**

- **The teacher is justified in giving the student a zero because he clearly identified the pen and pencil rule in the class guidelines.**

- **The teacher's guidelines are unnecessarily harsh because they punish the student by denying him a chance to demonstrate his knowledge.**

Discussion of this case study on page 205

CASE STUDY #11

THE INTERVIEW TRAP

You arrive at a school to interview for a job that you feel is an ideal teaching opportunity. The interview goes well at the outset; your preparation allows you to answer quickly and concisely.

After a half hour, the principal abruptly asks, "Are you married?" Taken aback, you ponder the question. Before you can answer, the principal says, "Imagine you are the principal. Two of my married faculty members are having an affair, and the whole school knows about it. What would you do if you were the principal? In other words, what do you think of faculty members committing adultery?"

How would you respond?

Discussion of this case study on page 207

Chapter 3:

Years One and Two:
Probationary Period -- Trials, Tears and Triumphs

The fourth thing you must know to become a master teacher:

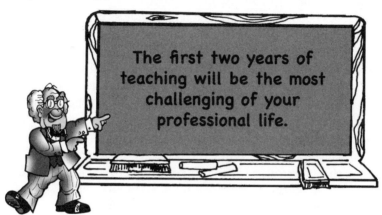

The first two years of teaching will be the most challenging of your professional life.

Contract signed, apartment rented, teaching assignment and room assignment determined–even with all that resolved, you have little idea how wild the first two years of teaching will be. Roughly one in five teachers leaves after the first two years, and nearly fifty percent leave within five years. Why? I think several factors contribute to the immense challenges in the first two years: abbreviated professional preparation, comparatively difficult teaching assignments, insufficient support, and excessive micromanagement from a number of school bureaucrats. Ironically, many recent efforts to improve student achievement have actually hindered new teacher retention because of the increased time out of the classroom for inservice and increased demands for documentation. Let me briefly address the above issues before discussing the crucial first two years.

Abbreviated professional preparation: Colleges and universities that include degrees in elementary and secondary education generally do excellent jobs of preparing students for their first positions. The standard curriculum followed by classroom observation, and then student teaching provides a logical and gradual immersion into teaching. But the next stage, full-time employment, presents a significant shift in expectations and responsibilities. Ideally, education should provide an internship period for beginning teachers to bridge the gap between student teaching and full-time teaching. I have seen too many idealistic and industrious young teachers leave the classroom after one or two years, feeling that they failed because all students did not achieve the success they envisioned for them. With an internship period, these talented young educators might have stayed in the profession and become master teachers. These challenging first two years highlight the need for a network of support in our schools which includes district administrators, building administrators, mentors and fellow teachers. We must not be a profession that consumes its young.

Comparatively difficult teaching assignments: Like most hierarchical professions, teaching possesses some assignments which are more attractive than others. Generally, classes for students who perform above grade level are more rewarding and more easily managed than classes for students who perform below grade level. The same applies to an assignment in an affluent suburb as opposed to an inner city school. New teachers often receive "entry level" assignments, a euphemism for classes with challenged learners. While some argue that this is not fair, that the new teachers should have less stressful assignments in their first years, the fact is that other young teachers begin with less than perfect assignments, and, through retirement and attrition, gradually assume the teaching loads that they prefer. During my first two years of high

"Children today are tyrants. They contradict their parents, gobble their food, and tyrannize their teachers."   *- Socrates (420 BC)*

school teaching, I traveled to four different classrooms every day, and nine of my ten classes were composed of students who performed below grade level. I do not see an immediate solution to this. People entering jobs in business do not enter as CEOs. People entering the military do not enter as four star generals. As teachers gain experience and advanced education, they may rightfully assume teaching assignments for advanced learners. The challenges of the first two years, the baptism of fire, provide new teachers with a realistic vision of teaching, which allows them to decide rather quickly if they want to pursue teaching as a profession.

Insufficient support: Unless schools have mentoring programs, teaching teams, or paired assignments, the first years of teaching can be painfully lonely. Young teachers are reluctant to admit that they have problems or that they feel powerless. Teachers entering a district without the above support systems must seek out other teachers in whom to confide.

Excessive micromanagement: In the twenty-first century, teachers live with benchmarks, standards, and competencies on local, state, and national levels. For new teachers, these externally imposed demands create tremendous stress. I know. I witness it every year I mentor another new teacher. The education community should realize that student achievement will not improve if committed young teachers leave the profession because they cannot manage the mountains of paperwork which prevent them from completing their lesson plans and focusing on the students they teach.

I cannot begin this section without recounting my first day in the classroom in August, 1975. I was twenty-four, fresh out of a successful student teaching stint that spring at a school similar to Dubuque Senior High. As I sat alone in the classroom that morning, I was terrified. Would the students rebel? Would I have classes full of discipline problems? Would I simply forget what I had planned? Would they laugh at me? When the warning bell rang, I was near panic. A few students came, quietly staring at me, and my anxiety rose with each new body. Two minutes before the bell, a colleague stuck his head in the door, smiled, and said, "You are going to be great!" What a relief. In one short sentence, he erased my fears. I never forgot it. When I train teachers to be mentors, I tell that story to underscore the angst of new teachers and the importance of support, and I stop by the first day to give them a smile and a vote of confidence.

"One man practicing sportsmanship is far better than a hundred teaching it."
- Knute Rockne

Despite these obstacles, many strong young teachers navigate the first two years safely. What follows is a survival guide of sorts, consisting of nine key areas:

- Self knowledge
- Knowledge of students
- Knowledge of colleagues
- Knowledge of administrators
- Knowledge of special programs
- Planning and record keeping
- Parent conferences
- Out-of-classroom issues
- Classroom management

SELF KNOWLEDGE

Before you teach the first class, reflect on how you conducted yourself during student teaching. Make adjustments based on your evaluation and your own reflections. Do this before the year starts; it's too difficult to transform yourself with students after certain patterns emerge. Know that this experience differs from student teaching in several key areas: one, you are the one, there's no backup; two, this is a yearlong commitment, not a ten or twelve week one; three, this time you are under contract.

Decide how you want to look and act, and make that statement the first time you face a class. There's an old saying, "Don't smile until Christmas," obviously dated with the reference to the holiday, and although hyperbolic, it's not such bad advice. As I stated in the student teaching section, it's fine to be serious at first, then loosen up later. It's also a good idea to look older (refer to the student teaching section which deals with personal appearance).

In the first years, you are not a divided self like you were as a student teacher: **you are a teacher**. I told a new teacher at our school recently to wear a tie every day. He was twenty-two, but appeared to be no more than eighteen. He thanked me at the end of the year.

KNOWLEDGE OF STUDENTS

It is crucial to know your students' names quickly, because you won't have time to observe in class like you did during student teaching. Several years ago, our governor chaired the first Iowa Summit on Education, and the most important thing I took from that day was his tripartite theme: Rigor, Relevance, and **Relationships**. Learn your students' names as quickly as possible. Take your class lists home and study them. I remember one of my college professors took pictures of each of us on the first day of the semester holding placards with our names on them, and the next time we met, he knew all of our names, and remembered them for the rest of the semester. Find a way that works for you.

For elementary and middle school teachers, know who is in stable families, who is moving from home to home, who lives with uncles, aunts, or foster parents. For high school teachers, know who is in music, who is in drama, who works forty hours a week, who baby-sits after school, who is on probation, who is behind in credits, who is applying to MIT, Harvard, and Vanderbilt, and who their siblings are. If you check on student transcripts, do not doom students to the self-fulfilling prophecy of stereotyping them so rigidly that you expect them either to succeed or fail based on previous performances and backgrounds. In my classes, all students start with a blank slate; I consider only their performances in my class as measures of their success.

"Furious activity is no substitute for understanding."
- H.H. Williams

Use student records as a challenge to make all students better by the time they leave your class, regardless of where they begin.

As with student teaching, knowing students outside of the classroom deepens your knowledge of them and their respect of you. I'm not advocating the typical scenario which so often unfolds in movies about teachers: the single teacher who has unlimited time outside of the classroom to make home visits, visits to jail or probation officers, or has students visit her/his apartment/home to resolve an unlimited number of problems more typically suited to mental health professionals. Sadly, motion picture producers and directors perform a disservice to hard-working teachers by suggesting that the only truly caring teachers are those who have no boundaries between their jobs and their personal lives. This is not the way the world works.

Be reasonable with your time. Make sure that if you have unstructured time, reserve some of it to attend school functions or situations in which you can see your students in non-classroom roles. Your seeing them and their seeing you makes a world of difference.

I have gone to some extreme lengths in my career to connect with students. In the mid-80's, I took a van full of high school students from Dubuque, Iowa, to Chicago, Illinois, to see Ozzy Osbourne and Anthrax at the Rosemont Horizon. I originally agreed to chaperone a bus, but not enough students signed up, so I agreed to drive a van. I talked to all of the parents before we left. I was apprehensive. It was a long trip, but the concert was fun (I watched from the back of the arena with a security guard), and the students appreciated my efforts. I wouldn't advise this for everyone, but for me, the risk paid off. I got to see the concert for free!

KNOWLEDGE OF COLLEAGUES

Within a few days of my first year of teaching, I found a teacher with whom I could confide, and he became my unofficial mentor. Today, a number of states mandate mentoring programs, and hopefully, you won't have to find a mentor on your own. When properly administered and structured, these programs provide the essential link between the innocence of new teachers and the experience of established teachers. Ideally, they hasten new teachers' development and their assumption of a professional persona. If you have such a program in your school district, take full advantage of it. In the best of all possible worlds, your mentor will become a valued colleague and role model. I have mentored eight new teachers since our district initiated its mentoring program in 1999, and

"Success is the sum of small efforts - repeated day in and day out."   *- Robert Collier*

I feel a special bond with them. Mentoring strengthens the relationships within a school; it builds morale; it benefits both mentor and mentee. Cultivate the relationship with your mentor—ask frequent questions, come to her/him in crisis, reflect on lessons, discuss discipline issues, inquire about other staff who may be of assistance, and share your triumphs. Don't walk alone in the first two years of teaching. If, however, your mentor match doesn't work out, contact the person who coordinates the program as soon as you feel the match is not working. A third party can either mend the match or find you another.

Hopefully, you will begin teaching with several other new teachers. Forming a bond with these teachers can be crucial because they will experience the same stresses as you and can share those feelings. Talking after school, going out for coffee, or having dinner together creates a peer support group which can be incredibly sustaining.

"*I have learned silence from the talkative, toleration from the intolerant, and kindness from the unkind; yet strange, I'm ungrateful to these teachers.*" *- Kahlil Gibran*

While the mentor and your fellow new teachers form your most significant professional peer group, you will be surprised who comprises the next level of the hierarchy of important colleagues. I consider all staff members colleagues, because all contribute to the success of the school. Aside from your mentor, your most important allies are the print center staff, the media specialist, the custodians, and the secretarial staff in various areas of the building. Do not ever, and I repeat, do not ever, act in a condescending or patronizing manner to any of these colleagues.

The print center staff will rescue you on last-minute orders which could make or break your lessons for that day.

The media specialist can find a DVD, a reference book, organize a collection of books on a topic you may be researching, order something from interlibrary loan, or help with the most efficient methods of ordering non-print materials for your classroom.

The custodians can fix the leak that suddenly comes from the roof, clean up the spilled soda in the hallway outside of your room, stop the overflowing drinking fountain some inconsiderate student plugged up over the lunch hour, or regulate the heat on a cold winter's day.

The secretaries will help locate student addresses and phone numbers, send materials for you, schedule appointments with administrators, find students during the day, and let you know what current discipline and attendance issues certain students face.

You want to survive? Treat the support staff with respect always!

"Courage is not the absence of fear, but rather the judgment that something else is more important than fear."
- Ambrose Redmoon

If you want to be uppity because you are a teacher and the support staff is "not on your level," expect to do a lot for yourself. In fact, you should consider finding some other line of work where you can get away with arrogance; it has no place in a school.

KNOWLEDGE OF ADMINISTRATION

Depending on the size of the school, leadership may fall to a single person, the principal, or a principal and an administrative team. Principals are the leaders of their buildings, and it is crucial for new teachers to become familiar with the personae, styles, and demeanors of the building leaders. They set the tone for the building, and your sense of comfort depends on how you fit in with the building's culture. An administrator will also be your primary evaluator, the one person who signs the forms signifying your suitability or unsuitability for the teaching profession. I have three recommendations for establishing and developing a relationship with the principal of your school:

First, make your initial interactions informal and positive. Principals are busy people, and few have much time for small talk. However, a quick minute of conversation in the hallway, the cafeteria, or the main office, imbued with enthusiasm and confidence, will establish a positive impression from which you can build.

Second, be fully informed about the evaluation process. States have differing policies, but most include the following: informal and formal observations; follow-up meetings to discuss the observations; documentation of competencies by the teacher, sometimes in the form of a portfolio; and, at the end of the observation period, what is known in educationese as a summative evaluation. A summative evaluation is an administrator's final statement regarding the new teacher's performance, usually identified as satisfactory, marginal (and needs to make specific improvements, usually in the next year, in order to "pass" the probationary period), or unsatisfactory and will not be retained.

Third, if at any time you feel uncomfortable with the evaluation process, schedule a meeting with the administrator and express your concerns. In most cases, you will be more worried than the administrator, who will assure you that things are going well. However, if you still feel uncertain, consult your mentor or someone you trust and identify the issue. These experienced teachers will help you decide if you need to take other action.

"To me education is a leading out of what is already there in the pupil's soul."
                                                                 - Muriel Sparks

Without doubt, the first evaluations are stressful. The second most traumatic moment of my first year of teaching (I will refer to the most traumatic moment later in this chapter) occurred when my primary evaluator made his first formal visit to my classroom. I stumbled through the lesson, looking at my evaluator more than my students. I was so flustered that I misspelled the word "mischief," on the blackboard, leaving out the "e". After the class, I noticed it as I erased the board. I thought I would be fired. After all, an English teacher who can't spell obviously doesn't know the subject. Later that day, I went to the administrator's office and apologized for the error. Without flinching, he said, "Just correct it for the students tomorrow." As I walked out, he said, "That won't be the last time you misspell a word on the board." He was right!

KNOWLEDGE OF SPECIAL PROGRAMS

Through your course work in college and in the observation and student teaching experiences, you will learn about programs designed to meet the needs of both challenged and highly capable students. Although titles change frequently, I will refer to the two major areas as Special Education and Talented and Gifted Education. Whether you are an elementary, middle school, or high school teacher, you will almost certainly have students who are in programs. The following list of reminders should allow you to understand the structure and function of these programs.

SPECIAL EDUCATION

Current trends: In the first decade of the twenty-first century, special education programs are evolving rapidly. National standards set by the No Child Left Behind Act have resulted in a shift from self-contained classrooms to inclusion (the dispersing of special education students into regular classrooms), and the reassignment of some special education teachers to co-teaching or team teaching with regular education teachers. Special education teachers should be aware of these changes, and the changing certification needs for special education.

Communication with staff and teams: Teachers who have special education students in their classrooms must maintain regular communication with the students' primary special education teachers. Regular communication (usually via e-mail) provides needed updates for the special education teacher, who can then work with the students on assignment completion, test preparation, and reading challenges. Regular education teachers are also required to attend staffings to ensure the students' educational progress. By all means, keep thorough records not only on grades, but also on communications with staff.

Your attitude: Perhaps the most important ingredient in successfully teaching special education students is your attitude toward them and the program. I taught mainstreamed special education students for over twenty years, and I challenged them as I would any other students while at the same time taking into consideration the circumstances surrounding their placement. Most of my students came from our learning

"If you want happiness for a lifetime, help someone else."
- Chinese proverb

disabilities and behavior disorders programs, and their teachers did a great job of preparing them for mainstreaming. Together our greatest successes involved motivating students to outgrow their labels, graduate, and continue their education. Some of the most satisfying moments of my career came from teaching these students.

TALENTED AND GIFTED

Current trends: Placement of Talented and Gifted (TAG) students takes various forms at each educational level. In elementary education, TAG students are frequently in pullout programs to receive differentiated instruction, usually by a specialist. In middle school and high school, specific subject matter teachers select these students for accelerated and enriched instruction. On the high school level, the growth in Advanced Placement courses throughout the United States has spawned vertical teams of teachers in grades 9-12 that prepare students for the rigor of AP classes in the upper grades. New teachers should have taken course work on TAG students to understand the academic and emotional support needed to work successfully with this population. If your building has a TAG coordinator, communicate regularly your questions and concerns.

Placement: Understand how your school places and schedules TAG students. Your school may have either a flexible or a rigid philosophy regarding placement, which may affect class size and makeup.

Parents: Parents of TAG students can be either the most supportive or the most combative, depending on their attitudes toward their children. In the first years in the classroom, avoid being intimidated by aggressive TAG parents by working with your building TAG coordinator and other appropriate staff. On occasion there are discrepancies between parents' perception of their children's giftedness and their children's performances, which can lead to unpleasant interactions. Avoid these situations by taking a team approach to TAG issues. You may need all the help you can get!

Your own attitude and philosophy: Since TAG students generally perform well in school, they tend to feel more positive about school. It is as important to nurture a TAG student's love of learning as it is to instill confidence in a special education student. The greatest common factor in teaching both of these student populations is the enthusiasm and vigor with which you approach instruction and the interest you take in them as learners and people. Ironically, some teachers reduce their efforts for both groups because they feel the special education students are limited in their learning capacity and that TAG students are smart anyway and can teach themselves. Nothing replaces passion in the classroom, regardless of who sits in the desks in front of you.

PLANNING AND RECORD KEEPING

A crucial part of your success in the first two years centers on organizational skills, specifically lesson planning and record keeping. I can't overemphasize how important it is to maintain order in the chaotic beginning of your career. There is a great deal to be said about leaving the classroom at day's end, turning, and seeing order and regularity even if your lesson plans are not complete or you are dealing with classroom management issues. It's reassuring, it's soothing, it's visual proof that you are in control of something. Most importantly, it shows closure: you have organized papers to read, reviewed absences and makeup work, laid out tasks to complete the next morning, made notes of people to see, people to e-mail, people to call. Avoid sloppiness at all costs. Sloppiness leads to mistakes, some of which could get you in big trouble.

One teacher I knew had a terrible time staying organized. Once I visited her room and she had old, graded student tests sitting on her desk. She had confidential memos lying in plain sight next to her computer. She had an answer key to a unit test openly displayed on a table she used to stack materials. You can imagine the problems inherent in such lax habits. The old saying, "A place for everything, and everything in its place," is good to take to heart in the first years of teaching. To me, this is a crucial part of being professional; taking pride in what you do includes managing your workspace. Being organized also prevents violation of privacy issues, theft of tests, and loss of time.

"A gifted teacher is as rare as a gifted doctor, and makes far less money."   *- Anonymous*

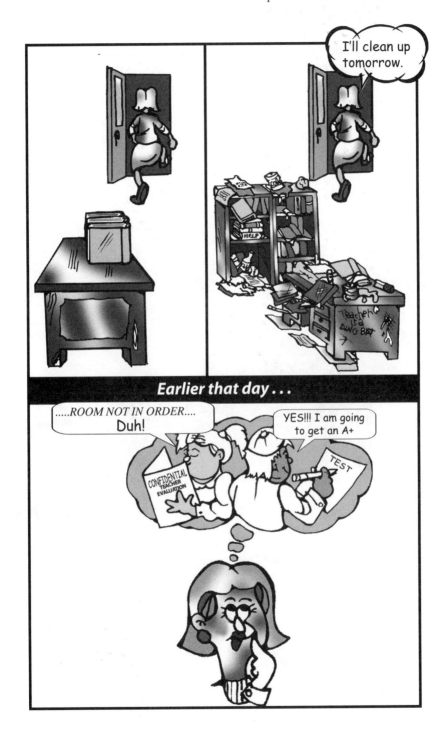

Lesson Planning: One of the most heavily scrutinized areas of student teaching is lesson planning. If you excelled in that area during student teaching, the transition to planning for a full teaching load will involve more time, but will require only minor adjustments. If, on the other hand, you struggled with planning (not writing down all you did, losing plans, not pacing the lessons according to the time listed in the plans, having trouble with closure), address the issues from day one.

"Develop a passion for learning. If you do, you'll never cease to grow."
                                                    - Anthony D'Angelo

Most schools require new teachers to submit lesson plans on a periodic basis, usually weekly or biweekly, to verify that the teacher is teaching the curriculum in a timely manner. I strongly recommend that you do the following seven things:

- Get a copy of the curriculum for your grade or courses before school starts and read it from beginning to end so that you know both the journey and the destination.

- Find your grade-alike or course-alike colleagues before the school year begins and go over questions or concerns you have about the curriculum.

- Buy a plan book if the school doesn't supply one and record all lesson plans. Your school may require you to send plans via e-mail, but it's good to have a hard copy at your disposal (on your desk) and not confined to a computer.

- Review and reflect on the lessons you teach. The Educational Testing Services (ETS) Pathwise program, which our school district uses in its mentoring program, has a useful sequence for the instructional process: Plan, Teach, Reflect, Apply. For new teachers, the reflection phase is helpful in refining lessons–building on strengths, adjusting in less successful areas–crucial to improvement in the first two years.

- Modify or make notes to modify lessons as soon as possible. Because of the need to plan for the next day, new teachers often fail to identify the changes they need to make. Consequently, they repeat the less-than-optimal lesson the next time through.

- Overplan. In the first two years, stay at least one day ahead with full plans. If you can get farther, by all means do so. But remember, in the first two years, you will make more modifications than you will in ensuing years. Specific long-range planning may not be the most efficient practice considering the number of changes you make.

- Have clear class guidelines and procedures. The old saying, "You never have a second chance to make a first impression" applies here. Establish yourself on the first day of class by providing students with an unambiguous list of classroom rules which are fair and defensible. I include a positive statement at the end of my guidelines, which sets the tone for me and my students. On the next page I have attached a copy of the class guidelines for one of the classes I teach:

CONTEMPORARY LIT. CLASS GUIDELINES AND PROCEDURES
MR. HEALY

MATERIALS: Since we do not have a textbook for this class, you must always bring pen or pencil, your notebook, and the assigned reading and/or writing materials to class. **Keep all notebooks, purses, etc. off the desk.**

ASSIGNMENTS: There are no pop quizzes in this class. I will announce all due dates for reading and writing assignments. It is in your best interest to have your work done on time. I will handle late work in the following manner:

    1-2 days late: 10% deduction
    3-4 days late: 20% deduction
    5 and beyond: 30% deduction

All major papers for this class must be word-processed. We will have time in the writing center to work on written assignments.

MAKEUP WORK: If you miss class, talk to me the day you return and we will determine your makeup schedule. If you miss a test and attended class the day before, you will take the test the day you return.

ATTENDANCE: Attendance is important to me, and it will be to your future employers. You can't learn if you are not here. I will keep accurate attendance records, and if I perceive a problem, I will talk to you. I will also follow the school's attendance policies.

TARDIES: Be in the room *when the bell rings.* We will start class on time. I will keep track of tardies. On the fifth tardy, you will lose five points. Each succeeding tardy will result in an additional point deducted from your grade.

SLEEPING: There will be no sleeping in class under any circumstances. Do not rest your head on your desk. If problems persist, we will discuss your sleep deprivation with the nurse.

FOOD AND BEVERAGES: Only water will be allowed in the classroom. No other food or beverages will be allowed.

CELL PHONES AND PAGERS: Cell phones and pagers must be shut off during class time.

GUIDANCE: Class time is not to be used for visits to guidance. If you have an emergency, come to class and I will make the necessary arrangements for you. If you visit guidance during class without seeing me first, I will consider it an unexcused absence.

DISMISSAL: Stay in your seat until the bell rings.

GRADES: I will operate two grading scales. If you attend class regularly and contribute to the class, you will use Grading Scale A; if you receive an unexcused absence, disrupt class, or accumulate ten non-medical or emergency absences, you will use grading scale B. They are listed below:

Scale A:		Scale B:		
91-100	A	93-100	A	40%--exams
83-90	B	85-92	B	25%--essays
73-82	C	75-84	C	15%--quizzes
63-72	D	65-74	D	10%--study questions
62 and below	F	64 and below	F	10%--notebook

MY ROLE AS A TEACHER: I believe that my main responsibilities as a teacher are to create an environment in the class which allows students to feel safe so they can learn, to establish good relationships with my students, and to do whatever I can to make you successful. In my class, I want to inspire a desire to learn by connecting the materials we study with the world you live in and the lives you lead. I will do my best \ every day to make class meaningful.

"It is not the answer that enlightens, but the question."
- Eugene Ionesco Decouvertes

Planning takes a lot of work, and sometimes seems to be tedious and repetitive. However, having the first two years of lesson plans documented and modified gives you a base from which to build a stronger teaching repertoire.

Planning for a Substitute Teacher: Writing clear lesson plans is a courtesy every teacher should provide for substitutes. I wrote this lesson plan for a long weekend I took one year. Imagine the substitute knows nothing about your classes or curriculum when you construct lesson plans. Give detailed directions and plan for entire class periods. Read the lesson to yourself after drafting it to see if you could follow it! Consult your school's guidelines for lesson plans for substitutes and follow them closely.

LESSON PLANS   APRIL 13 AND 18

Kristina, Thanks so much for taking my classes. Here is the important info:

Schedule: P. 1: Prep
             P. 2: AP English
             P. 3: Contemporary Lit.
             P. 4: AP English
             P. 5: AP English   (study A 11:04-11:24; class 11:24-12:10; lunch
                                    12:10-12:38)
             P. 6: Supervision   Write Place
             P. 7: Department Chair

AP classes do not have seating charts. Contemporary Lit. seating chart is in the red folder.

NOTE: WE ARE ASSEMBLY SCHEDULE FOR THURSDAY. YOU WILL SIT WITH THE 4TH PERIOD STUDENTS UNDER THE PRESS BOX.

LESSON PLANS

Contemporary Lit.
    Thursday: These student will have a shortened period. Hand out the questions for Chapters 5-7. Students will work on these questions for the period. If you want to discuss them in the final 10 minutes, go ahead. Circulate during class time to ensure that students are working on the assignment. If you discuss the chapters, focus on Holden's idealizing of Allie, his violent reaction to his death, his violent reaction to Stradlater's rejection of his essay and his snide remarks about his date with Jane, the fight which Holden loses, his suicidal ideation in chapter 7, and his ultimate decision to escape from Pencey.
    If students have their section summary done for chapters 1-7, collect them, mark the date, and paper clip them together.

    Tuesday: Similar to Thursday's lesson, distribute the questions for chapters 8-9. Give students time to work and read, then discuss the questions for those chapters. Focus on the lies Holden tells Mrs. Morrow, the reason why he lies, his failure to communicate in the phone booth at the beginning of chapter 9, and his ambivalence about sex (he sees the perverts, but it is he who is the voyeur; he claims to respect women, then calls a woman who may be "available"; he wants to see her, then tells her he can't meet her the next day even though he has nothing to do). This chapter shows how confused Holden is.

    Do not collect these sheets; they are for their notes and for discussions.

AP Lit.:
    Thursday: These students will take a multiple choice portion of a released AP

"The whole art of teaching is only the art of awakening the natural curiosity of young minds."

- Anatole France

exam. After attendance, have the students scramble, then hand out clean Scantron sheets to each student. Tell them to answer on spaces 46-55. Give them 12 minutes to answer, then collect the scantron forms. Take the forms to the AV area (I've notified the AV people to assist you), run them through (you'll have to scan both sides!), return them to the students and discuss the questions. If you have time left, hand out the items to consider for <u>Things Fall Apart</u>. This sheet will be the basis of the students' work on Tuesday. Collect the Scantron forms at the end of the period and paper clip them.

Tuesday: Today, these students will work on the items to consider for <u>Things Fall Apart</u>. They may work in pairs, and they must generate written responses to each question. This should easily take the entire period. Let them know that I expect to discuss the questions on Wednesday. There is a sheet for each student. Do not have students hand them in.

Again, thanks for taking over. If you have questions, three of my colleagues are right next door in room D-155. They will be happy to help you. I will also write the plans for the day on the board for both Thursday and Tuesday. Please erase before you leave on Tuesday.

Dennis

Record Keeping: The most traumatic moment of my first year of teaching occurred at the end of the first quarter. For the entire quarter I had dutifully taken daily attendance, placed the attendance sheets on the hook on the door of the room, and taught my classes. I did not read my faculty handbook closely enough, because I was also supposed to keep attendance records of my own, and record cumulative absences on the grade sheets we received at the end of each quarter. When the end of the quarter arrived and I realized I had not kept attendance records, I panicked. Afraid to admit my error to the administration, I asked my unofficial mentor what to do. He said to go to the attendance office, tell the secretary, and ask for the attendance records. I did, and she was sympathetic. The problem was that there were no individual teacher records, only one alphabetized list for all students. On the last Friday of the quarter, she let me check out the list. I had to check all absences and tardies for the first forty-five days, pick out my students, and record them on the grade sheets, all in two days. Fortunately, I got it done, barely. What a nightmare!

"Spoon feeding in the long run teaches us nothing but the shape of the spoon."
- E.M. Forster

Three major points form the crux of record keeping:
- • Understand all of your school's procedures for keeping records.
- • Update your records regularly.
- • Maintain confidentiality.

Understand record-keeping procedures: To avoid having your own tale of woe, know exactly what documentation your school requires regarding grades, attendance, parent contacts, discipline notices, guidance referrals, and referrals to the school nurse. In today's computer-based, data-driven world, failure to have proper documentation can lead to anything from a mild rebuke from the administration to legal action from a distraught parent. Most of the important documentation in the first two years will find its way into your portfolio, but it's not a bad idea to save any communication which deals with student or parent matters.

Update records regularly and accurately: One of my colleagues is an outstanding teacher and coach. He gets extremely busy during his coaching seasons. Our fall parent-teacher conferences take place at the end of the cross country season, a time when he compiles an enormous amount of statistical information for the team's banquet. One season, he delayed entering some grades for his Advanced Placement Statistics Class until the last moment. In his haste, he entered his student comments in a space designated for a 100-point test. His comments, almost all positive, were all coded in very low numbers. For example, the comment, "Doing excellent work," had a corresponding number of 3. After dutifully entering these complimentary comments, however, in a column designated for a 100-point assignment, the students' grades plummeted, causing considerable confusion at his conference table. Thankfully, it was a correctable error. On the plus side, he had excellent attendance at his conferences!

With most schools now using electronic grading, entering data is a relatively easy task. But the longer you delay, the more likely it is that you will make errors, and with parents having greater access to their children's grades, it is even more important to establish a habit of swift and accurate entering of grades. If you enter data promptly, you can tell who has completed the work and who hasn't, who is improving and who isn't, and who may need a pep talk or a parent contact. You can also avoid the embarrassing e-mail from a parent asking why you haven't entered grades for two weeks!

"A teacher is one who makes himself progressively unnecessary."
- Thomas Carruthers

Maintain confidentiality: A friend of mine has children who attended the high school at which I teach. One semester at parent-teacher conferences, he asked a teacher for a more specific breakdown of his son's grade. The teacher, who did not have individual student grade material available, simply turned his grade book around and said to my friend, "Here, take a look for yourself." My friend not only got to see his son's individual grades, but also had access to the grades of the other twenty-five students in the class. He was shocked that the teacher was so casual about confidentiality. You must be more protective of student records than the above teacher.

Today, with so much data available on student performance, there is a greater danger that student information intended to be confidential becomes available to others. For example, teachers can now print individual student grade reports and distribute them to students. I have seen student grade reports left on student desks, in recycling bins, on floors in classrooms, in the halls, and in plain sight on teacher desks. To avoid unpleasant interactions, take precautions to ensure that anything of a confidential nature remains confidential. Shredding documents that are no longer valid or necessary is a good preventative measure. But the best insurance against violating confidentiality is being organized and being alert to the sensitivity of school materials.

Record keeping is a clerical task. Approach it with punctuality, professionalism, and sensitivity.

PARENT CONFERENCES

Although you participated in parent conferences during student teaching, the first experiences of talking to parents one-on-one can be as unsettling as they are rewarding. As a new teacher, you are vulnerable to parents who may question your knowledge and experience. To minimize these potentially uncomfortable encounters, prepare well. The seven guidelines that follow will minimize confrontation.

• Greet parents/guardians by standing, making eye contact, introducing yourself, shaking hands and thanking them for coming.

• Begin by making a positive comment about the student.

• Have a syllabus of the class for the parents/guardians to peruse and inform them about what you are currently studying.

• Have a printout of the student's grades and attendance to give to the parents/guardians. Study this information before conferences so you can make specific points about the student's strengths and areas in which the student needs to make a more concerted effort.

• Ask the parents/guardians if they have questions or concerns — avoid overreacting to criticism; rather, keep the discussion focused on the student's performance.

• If the parents/guardians become combative or belligerent, excuse yourself and seek out the nearest administrator or experienced teacher and inform that person of the situation. No teacher deserves to be browbeaten; be alert to personal attacks and be prepared to act swiftly.

• At the close of the conference, thank the parents/guardians for coming, stand, make eye contact, and shake their hands.

Parent conferences are exercises in diplomacy. Handle them deftly and you will have rewarding experiences.

OUT-OF-CLASS ISSUES

What you do with the time you don't teach also affects your professional development in the first two years of teaching. Keep these three things in mind:

• Make connections with students outside the classroom.
• Conduct yourself in a professional manner in the community.
• Manage weekends and vacations carefully so you will be more respected and less stressed.

Make connections outside the classroom: I will not repeat what I wrote in the student teaching chapter, but the same concept applies in the first two years: students develop more respect for you when you observe them in activities outside the classroom. In addition to attending events, you can now sponsor or cosponsor activities. Find something you enjoy and get involved, whether it is starting a book club, a service club, an environmental club, or assisting with an already-existing activity. Some teachers may dispute this, but teachers who sponsor clubs and activi-

---

"Successful teachers are effective in spite of the psychological theories they suffer under." — Educational proverb

ties in their schools invariably have a more positive attitude toward students and students have a more positive attitude toward them. The first steps toward becoming a master teacher are inextricably tied to a love of students and their development both inside and outside the classroom. There is no short cut here.

Conduct yourself in a professional manner in the community: Once you leave your classroom after school, the time is yours. But in a way, it isn't. "Out there" you are always a teacher. After over thirty years, I am aware of it every day. I have taught and/or coached over 5,000 students, and it is inevitable that I will encounter on every foray into town a former student, a current student, or a parent or parents of current or former students. Like it or not, your identity as a teacher grants you certain prestige. Conduct yourself knowing that you are watched as a person who works with young people, and be willing to accept that you are held to higher standards than people in other professions.

Manage weekends and vacations: Don't over schedule time off. The first years generate enough stress; you will work long hours, well beyond the forty-hour work week. Having time off will seem a luxury. If your hometown is within driving distance from where you teach, going home every weekend creates a disconnect from the school. It will be hard to attend activities, socialize with other teachers, and familiarize yourself with the community in which you now reside. Ask family and friends to visit you from time to time. Hopping in a car on Friday afternoon and returning late Sunday reduces both the time it takes to decompress from the week you just finished and to gear up for the week that lies ahead. Create a schedule that gives you time to relax.

Speaking of relaxing, be sure that your weekends are not too fun-filled. Partying from Friday afternoon until Sunday night is not best practice. I recall a former colleague who fell in love with a young woman who lived ninety miles away. He was in his late twenties, and he visited her every weekend. On several occasions, he returned on Monday morning, sometimes through a window rather than the front doors, looking a little rough

"Two kinds of teachers: The kind that fill you with so much quail shot that you can't move, and the kind that just give you a little prod behind and you jump to the skies."   **- Robert Frost**

and searching for lesson plans. Remarkably, he survived that ill-fated romance, now has a Ph.D., and is a distinguished teacher in a metropolitan area. He was lucky. Manage your time so that you can come to school every Monday with a clear mind and ready to teach.

CLASSROOM MANAGEMENT

Formal evaluators place their greatest emphasis on classroom management during your first two years of teaching. It is a major part of the formal evaluation process, and crucial to your ability to deliver effective lessons.

I have touched on classroom management issues in Chapter One and in this chapter. On the following pages is a summary of the points I have made, based on my career in the classroom and my ten years of mentoring new teachers.

HEALY'S KEYS TO
SUCCESSFUL CLASSROOM MANAGEMENT

 Start class on time every day.

 State your concern for student success on the first day.

 State your expectations and rules clearly on the first day.

 Make connections from the first day.
   Learn students' names as soon as possible.
   Establish a relationship with each student as soon as possible.

 Place lesson plans on the board every day.

 Maintain a diversified method of delivering lessons.

 Pace daily lessons, emphasizing introductions, transitions, and conclusions.

 Maintain a sense of humor.

 Do not favor any students; be consistent in every facet of instruction.

 Do not confront students directly in front of their peers; discuss individual issues one-on-one.

 Make discipline referrals to the principal as infrequently as possible.

 Manage your class; let it not manage you.

"Teaching should be such that what is offered is perceived as a valuable gift and not as a hard duty."   *- Albert Einstein*

Return assignments as quickly as possible.

 Keep students apprised of their performances and their grades.

 Praise the class for jobs well done.

 Make lessons as rigorous and relevant as possible.

 Express disappointment in a positive way *(emphasize that you expect better efforts).*

 Value every student even if not every student values you.

CONCLUSION

The primary focus of your first two years as a teacher is to successfully complete the probationary period and lay the groundwork for even greater future successes. See yourself as the young professional you are, and conduct yourself accordingly. Above all, teach your heart out; give all you have to your students in the most rigorous, but positive and supportive manner you can. When you reach the end of the first two years and say to yourself, "I did it," add, "Now let's see how good I can be!" The next stage in becoming a master teacher will give you that opportunity. Seize it!

CASE STUDY #12

SUPERVISION

You supervise one of your school's computer labs. It is an active area. Teachers bring classes in to work on essays, do internet research, and create power point presentations. You also supervise individual students who come to the computer lab to work on assignments for other teachers.

Your supervision is the last period of the day. One Friday, a science class works on an internet assignment on endangered species, using twenty-five of the thirty computers. Two "walk-ins," students with passes from their teachers to make up late work, are also busy.

At the end of the period, all students leave except one. As you check to see that all computers are logged off, the student continues to work.

You tactfully tell him that the period is over and that you must close the computer lab. He asks you to let him stay to finish his assignment, which is already late. He says he's almost finished, and adds that he has no computer at home and will not be able to finish the assignment unless he stays.

What do you do?

- **Stay with him until he finishes, even though you have other commitments?**

- **Tell him that his teacher must supervise him because the school has no after-school program, and that you will call the teacher's room and ask her to come to the lab?**

- **Tell him he must leave, because you cannot allow students to be in the computer lab unsupervised?**

- **Tell him that he can stay, but he must turn off the lights and close the door tightly when he leaves?**

Discussion of this case study on page 209

CASE STUDY #13

PROBLEM SOLVING WITH THE PRINCIPAL

Parent teacher conferences are a stressful time for teachers. On all levels—elementary, middle school, and high school—teachers can work for hours without a break seeing parent after parent or guardian after guardian. While most conferences go well, the teacher never knows how parents will react to their children's performances and the teacher's interpretation of those performances. One year at our high school during fall conferences, our principal decided to take the conference days off and go hunting with some friends in another part of the state.

When conferences started, teachers quickly learned that their principal was not there. After conferences ended, teachers complained about the principal's absence. The principal caught wind of these complaints and was quite upset.

He called me into his office to tell me that he was calling a faculty meeting to say that he had every right to take the days off and that he was tired of hearing about these whiners and complainers. He said people who were upset should tell him personally about it. I could tell he was angry and that the faculty meeting would be a dressing down session.

I believe I handled this session well.

What did I say to the principal?

Discussion of this case study on page 211

CASE STUDY #14

COMING TO THE AID OF A COLLEAGUE

A colleague of yours is in his early years in the classroom. He is also an activity sponsor. He takes a group of students to a state competition out of town. While he and the team are there, his fiancée stays with him at the hotel where he and the team are staying. In fact, she stays in the same room with him.

After the group performs and returns, the principal receives an anonymous telephone call informing him of the hotel situation. Two days later, the principal calls the teacher into his office and without warning, tells him that the school district plans to fire him.

You are also a young activities sponsor. The teacher comes to you and asks what he should do. You refer him to the representative of the local teachers' association.

In the meantime, other activities sponsors find out about the nature of the phone call and the abruptness of the meeting with the principal. People feel that the young teacher was not treated fairly.

What would you do in this situation?

- **Organize the other activities sponsors and register a protest to the superintendent?**

- **Let the teachers' association deal with it?**

- **Notify an attorney friend for advice?**

- **Side with the principal to show support of strong ethics?**

Discussion of this case study on page 213

CASE STUDY #15

THE JOURNAL NIGHTMARE

Journaling is a popular writing activity not only in the language arts, but also in other curricular areas as a means to enhance literacy and writing across the curriculum. There is a range of responses among journal writers, from the unresponsive to the indifferent to the competent to the highly verbal and analytical. Any of these groups can include students who are self-disclosing, sometimes to an alarming degree.

Imagine that early in your career you have a journaling requirement in your class. One student writes extensive and serious entries about the personal issues of her life—dating, her parents, her classes, her job, her weekends. One Thursday night as you settle in to read journals, you select hers. After a page of processing the week, she divulges that her parents are manufacturing, selling, and using methamphetamine and that life at home has become unbearable.

What is the first thing you do when you arrive at school the next morning?

- **Call the police?**

- **Take the journal to the guidance counselor?**

- **Call the girl's parents immediately?**

- **Find the girl in school and ask to speak to her?**

- **Report the incident to the school nurse and the assistant principal?**

Discussion of this case study on page 215

CASE STUDY #16

EXCESSIVE VISITS TO GUIDANCE

You have a large class, and managing attendance is challenging. Midway into the first marking period, you notice that a certain student comes to class late at least once a week with a pass from his guidance counselor. You also discover that on several past occasions when the student was absent, he spent the entire period with his counselor. You notice no demonstrable emotional problems with the student, and he completes his work, but has fallen behind because of the time he spends with his counselor.

What do you do?

- **Complain to the principal?**

- **Talk to the student to find out why he misses so much class?**

- **Talk to the guidance counselor to find out if the student has some problem of which you are unaware?**

- **Confront the guidance counselor and demand that the student not miss any more class time?**

- **Call the student's parents to report the tardies and absences and inform them that the student's grade has fallen because of the visits to the counselor?**

Discussion of this case study on page 217

CASE STUDY #17

THE INATTENTIVE STUDENT

You are a middle school math teacher. As you present a lesson on a new concept, you notice a student sitting near the back reading a book. This student is highly proficient in math, and when you ask the student to put away the book and pay attention, he says he already knows the concept.

What do you do at that point?

- **Say immediately, "It doesn't matter, put your book away" ?**

- **Allow the student to continue to read, then talk to him individually after class?**

- **Send the impudent student to the principal' office?**

- **Throw an eraser at him to get his attention?**

- **None of the above?**

Discussion of this case study on page 219

Chapter 4:

Years Three through Ten: Committing to a Career in the Classroom Through Professional Development and Advanced Degrees

The fifth thing you must know to become a master teacher:

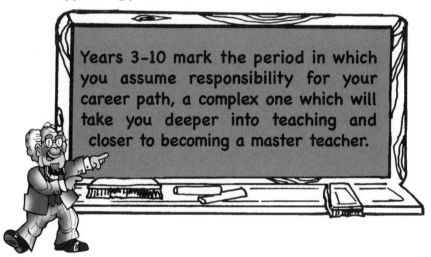

Years 3-10 mark the period in which you assume responsibility for your career path, a complex one which will take you deeper into teaching and closer to becoming a master teacher.

Teaching is a strange profession. During the probationary period, you undergo intense scrutiny from the administration, and you establish a close working relationship with your mentor if your district provides one. If you receive a satisfactory summative evaluation at the end of this period, you suddenly enter a phase of your career that places you essentially on your own. You will be evaluated only periodically, and the formal mentoring period ends. The irony of this situation is that during the years 3-10, you will make many critical decisions that will affect the rest of your career. This period will be one of tremendous professional and personal growth.

In this chapter, I will identify seven major issues you will face during years 3-10, and offer suggestions that will allow you to deal with them professionally and honestly. The major areas I will touch on are as follows:

- Post-probationary letdown
- Setting goals
- Personal and professional life changes
- Changing professional roles
- Crafting your craft and building your reputation
- Community involvement
- Monitoring and managing stress

"When teaching, light a fire, don't fill a bucket."   *- Dan Snow*

POST-PROBATIONARY LETDOWN

As the previous illustration indicates, the contrast between the considerable oversight of your probationary period and the independence you gain in the next phase of your teaching career can leave you with a sense of loneliness and isolation. While the classroom visits, portfolio building, and mentoring events of the probationary period may have become tedious as you grew more confident in those first two years, the absence of support and feedback can be disconcerting. You'll still have questions, challenges, and moments of uncertainty.

To overcome this shift, keep the lines of communication open with any or all of the following: your mentor, your grade-alike or course-alike colleagues, another teacher in whom you can confide, a trusted administrator, and your spouse, significant other, or your closest friend. Whether or not your district requires it, continue to build your portfolio to document your growth. In the absence of formal evaluation, a growing portfolio is a personal way to bolster confidence and to see your career developing.

If your relationship with your mentor was amicable, productive and based on trust, there is no reason for the connection to end. In fact, it can grow, and you can become peers. The first teacher I mentored and I are still close. We share a course assignment, and communicate daily, sharing ideas and making suggestions for new materials. We also occasionally meet for Friday "Staff Meetings," which consist of school talk on a less formal basis at an off-school site. The mentor-to-peer relationship can become one of the strongest bonds you forge as a teacher.

Grade-alike and/or course-alike colleagues can provide daily interactions which foster sustained communication. They may grow into partnerships and produce the continued professional growth which is so crucial in the post-mentoring years. Classroom management, lesson planning, materials selection, pacing, and dealing with general building issues will all be less stressful when you rely on a trusted colleague.

As I said before, I had no official mentor, but in my early years, I confided regularly with an experienced social studies teacher for whom I had great respect. He made time for me if I requested it, and his advice was nearly always helpful. Without his guidance, my path would have been much more difficult. Look around your school. It won't take too much time to figure out who is most respected and who provides the greatest leadership. Don't be afraid to approach these people; they can be invaluable resources.

If, by this time you are married or have a significant other, by all means share your experiences. An understanding partner can smooth the evening after a rough day. But be careful. The old saying, "Don't bring the job home with you," has some merit. Excessive complaining can become tiresome, and if it persists, it may create problems in your relationship. If you find yourself going home unhappy and stressed on a regular basis, consider counseling and/or therapy. Many school districts cover mental health counseling, and talking through your issues with a trained professional may not only save your job, but also your relationship. I got lucky; my wife is a psychologist, and without her, I wouldn't be writing this book.

"To waken interest and kindle enthusiasm is the sure way to teach easily and successfully."   *- Tyron Edwards*

SETTING GOALS

At this phase of my career, I realized that I needed to plan my future in the class-room, so I established some career goals. First, I returned to school to pursue a master's degree in English. Second, I wanted to continue coaching, but I did not want to coach during the winter or summer and I did not want to coach high-pro-file sports. When positions opened for track in the spring and cross country in fall, I applied for them and was hired. My wife and my unofficial mentor were my consultants in these decisions, and their advice was tremendously helpful.

Goal setting in years three through ten centers on educational advancement and co-curricular sponsorship. Let's examine those more closely.

Educational goals: For a career in the classroom, educational goals should focus on what will take you to the master teacher level. Whether you are an elemen-tary, middle school, or high school teacher, there are numerous master's level programs, some of which can be taken on the internet. It is good to explore all the possibilities in your area to find the most compatible in terms of location, tuition, and specificity of course offerings. Since much of the work will take place during the summer months, plan to set aside several summers to complete the degree. Pursue this degree as soon as it is feasible. Returning to school can be costly, especially if the closest institutions are private and you have no schol-arships or loans. Tuition costs, paying off student loans, and starting a family can put young career teachers in a bind. Weigh financial factors before making a decision, but I urge you to find a way to continue your education; you will lose money every year you delay, and you will delay an even more important step–becoming more skilled and knowledgeable in the classroom. Growing both pedagogically and emotionally paves the way toward mastery.

Co-curricular goals: Schools at all levels offer opportunities for teachers to sup-plement their incomes through activity sponsorship, from extended day activi-ties on the elementary level, to after school sports, music, and dramatic events on the middle school level, to coaching, directing plays and musicals, sponsor-ing debate teams, and coaching students for speech contests on the high school level. As I have said before, these commitments bring you closer to students and allow you to relate to students in ways that you cannot in the classroom. They can build a lifetime of memories. But they also take time. Weigh the benefits of activity sponsorship before signing contract addenda.

"He who dares to teach must never cease to learn."

- Anonymous

I coached for 28 years, and found it enriching and rewarding. Teaching made me a better coach, and coaching made me a better teacher. Today, six years after I retired from coaching, I still hear from former runners who want advice on training. When I ran the Chicago Marathon in October of 2005 to qualify for the Boston Marathon, a former runner recognized me as we awaited the start. We talked before the race and e-mailed afterward. When I ran the Boston Marathon in 2006, one of my former runners who also qualified, did a long training run with me a month before the race and rode on a bus with me to Hopkinton, where the marathon starts. Several other former runners found out I was running and sent me encouraging e-mails. I can't imagine anything more affirming.

Experiencing success can bring additional respect for you and the school. Our cross country teams qualified for the state meet eleven consecutive seasons. I know I was proud, but I also know that the young women I coached were proud, and sensed the tradition we established. No one wanted to be in the class that ended the streak. Success breeds confidence, which I believe carries over to the classroom and community. Do not underestimate the effects of being a successful activity sponsor.

A final note. One of the finest students I ever taught was also a runner. In the spring of 2006, she graduated from Stanford University in the top 5% of her class and selected me to represent her at a recognition luncheon on the Stanford campus. It was a proud moment, and I knew that the bond we forged both in the classroom and through running was the deciding factor in her selecting me. In fact, we ran together when I went to Stanford, and I got the best campus tour of all of the teachers who were honored!

Weigh the benefits and challenges of activity sponsorship before committing. If you are passionate and compassionate and have the time and desire, you can build some wonderful memories.

Our 1993 cross-country team after finishing 9ᵗʰ in the State Meet.

"I am almost overwhelmed by the courage and dedication of teachers."
                                                    - Sylvia Solomon

PERSONAL AND PROFESSIONAL LIFE CHANGES

Years three through ten present many possible life changes for the young career teacher. I have seen teachers marry, have children, divorce and remarry, take sabbaticals, work toward advanced degrees, become head coaches, get elected to site councils, become department chairs, leave teaching and come back to teaching, win awards for teaching, switch from secondary to elementary teaching and vice versa, switch disciplines, and transfer to other schools. These examples reveal the unpredictability of the teaching profession for those who make teaching a career. This period poses serious questions regarding family and finances.

What causes all the upheaval? Certainly, your personal life evolves in this stage. Settling into a professional career creates changes in your outlook.

Family: For one thing, you will look more toward the future. If you marry, having children, as wonderful as it is (my wife and I have two), places more demands on your daily routine. Keep your family in the forefront of your life. For me, the summers with my young children were priceless. I feel that the closeness that we have as a family comes from the time both my wife and I spent with our children when they were young. My wife did not enter the workforce until our second child entered kindergarten, and I eschewed employment in the summers to be with my children. While it limited our total income, it forged bonds that remain strong today. I was very busy during the school year with teaching and coaching, but I knew my children and they knew me. Find the balance you need to build your career and your family.

For example, suppose you sponsor an elementary after-school program funded by a grant that pays you for your efforts. The after school program raises test scores for students, wins awards, and brings publicity and respect to your school. This program, however, means that you don't arrive home until six p.m. four nights a week, and your children stay in daycare until that time. You may be torn between the students who are improving and your own children. Even if the daycare is good and your spouse is supportive, it is a tough decision, a Catch-22. Assess your entire family's well-being as you commit from year to year.

"The ones whom you should try to get even with are the ones who have helped you."   *- Anonymous*

Finances: Providing for a family costs money. At this point, I must address this issue. Teaching is not the most lucrative professional field of endeavor. As you can see by the history of my earnings (see following page), it is a challenge to support a spouse and children on only a teacher's salary, even with extra duty pay. Wages and benefits differ widely from state to state and district to district. There are numerous web sites which provide this information. Weigh the salaries and benefits issue as you plan the future for you and your family. As I mentioned earlier in this chapter, if you also return to school during this period, you will have to watch finances even more closely.   If you remain single or if your spouse also works outside of the home, you should be able to live comfortably. Above all, once you commit to a career in the classroom, find a way to overcome the monetary challenges which may delay your progress toward mastery.

"Surely the highest charge in teaching is to teach what we ourselves have loved."
- William Bennett

Calendar Year	Wage Summary
1975 *(partial year)*	$3,335.32
1976	$10,817.64
1977	$12,401.00
1978	$13,840.32
1979	$14,075.96
1980	$15,648.83
1981	$18,027.80
1982	$20,000.00
1983	$20,000.00
1984	$21,000.00
1985	$21,000.00
1986	$22,000.00
1987	$23,000.00
1988	$24,000.00
1989	$26,000.00
1990	$28,000.00
1991	$31,000.00
1992	$34,000.00
1993	$35,000.00
1994	$38,000.00
1995	$41,000.00
1996	$44,000.00
1997	$47,128.49
1998	$48,741.97
1999	$50,569.47
2000	$51,326.06
2001	$53,547.54
2002	$53,777.81
2003	$54,453.45
2004	$55,371.41
2005	$59,230.46
2006	$62,037.48

Finally, at this stage of your career, consider how you want to manage your finances. Do you want to go it alone? Do you want to consult a financial advisor? Do you want to find an insurance agent who can handle all your needs? Ask around your school and find out how teachers deal with their finances. Consult with your parents and trusted friends. Careful and wise financial management can inspire spending discipline in the early years of your career and give you security later in your career.

One final note on compensation. During this phase of your career, weigh the consequences of moving to another state. States have differing retirement systems, and by working in one state for a few years, then moving to another state, you may lose credit on your previous state's pension plan. These pensions are often not transferable from one state to another since they are established by individual states. If you move, you may receive a lump sum of money for your service, but you'll probably have to either start over on your credit for years of service on the salary schedule and/or lose some portion of your years of service toward your pension. This can result in your having to teach additional years beyond your desired retirement age in order to be fully vested in your new state's retirement system. If you are a career teacher, make a decision regarding location by your fifth year to ensure that you will not compromise the strength of your pension.

"You can always tell luck from ability by its duration."
                                              - Anonymous

CHANGING PROFESSIONAL ROLES

Becoming a master teacher involves more than becoming adept in the classroom. You must have an effect on your school outside of the classroom as well. See yourself as a consummate professional. To do that, stay abreast of contemporary issues in education and contribute to your school's mission and vision by involving yourself in groups, committees, or teams which explore such issues as local, state, and federal mandates and their effect on your school; restructuring issues such as changing special education requirements, block scheduling, smaller learning communities, and district mandated changes in curriculum and instruction; and technology issues and their effects on classroom instruction, parent communication, and record keeping. Finally, weigh the pros and cons of joining your local bargaining unit, association, or union.

Local, State, and National Mandates: In the first decade of the twenty-first century, the No Child Left Behind Act, national and state graduation requirements, entry level testing for new teachers, changes in teacher evaluation procedures, portfolio requirements for teachers, and changes in continuing education requirements affect teachers at all levels. If you want to have a voice in the administering of these initiatives, consider becoming involved at the building, district, or state levels. You may express the only teacher point of view on some committees, and administrators and district personnel may not have the perspective you do as a classroom teacher. By having a voice, being involved in these issues can shape your future teaching.

Restructuring Issues: Educational reform initiatives touch every generation of teachers. During my career I have seen schools within schools, the proliferation of Advanced Placement classes, the expansion of special education and the move from self-contained classrooms to mainstreaming, and the move toward interdisciplinary curricula. And that's just on the high school level. I've seen middle schools replace junior high schools and I've seen numerous elementary school changes–shifts to "whole language" followed by a return to more traditional language arts instruction; teachers teaching a specific grade level to teachers staying with students for two or more years and moving with students from grade to grade; and changes in conferencing and grade reporting.

"Humility does not mean you think less of yourself. It means you think of yourself less."
- Ken Blanchard

At this phase of your career, you will adapt to these changes if you understand their causes and effects. Subscribing to periodicals specific to your field, finding reliable web sites that cover school changes, and attending workshops that focus on the future of education will keep you in the forefront. If a particular initiative interests you, become involved by being a building representative. Recently, our school voted to establish small learning communities for our freshman class, putting over 400 freshmen into five "houses" to provide those freshmen with a transitional year into high school which has teachers work in teams to ensure students don't falter in the first year. Teachers in years three through ten spearheaded this change. It was impressive to work with them, and I witnessed their growing maturity, confidence, and sense of ownership in our school's future direction.

Change is not easy in schools, but when facilitated by positive, enthusiastic, and committed teachers, it benefits all. Don't be afraid to shape the future of your school.

Technology: Many of today's teachers in years three through ten are more knowledgeable and more comfortable with technology than those who are older. If you are adept with the forms of technology schools use, you can assume leadership roles early in your career. Opportunities exist for teachers to be tech mentors, to write grants, and to lead inservice sessions when technology changes. In an interesting reversal, several of the teachers I have mentored have mentored me in the uses of our computerized grading system, setting up a web site, and finding shortcuts for certain communication and storage functions. Being willing to assist with technology issues will allow you to develop collegial relationships with more experienced teachers who may teach at different grade levels or in different disciplines. You will also enhance your professional identity in the building by being seen as a go-to person for staff who need help.

A perfect example of younger teachers providing technological assistance occurred recently in our school. Our publications teacher came to school near the end of the school year to look at some of the final sections of our school's yearbook. When she opened the hard drive, none of the yearbook information appeared! She asked a fourth-year teacher familiar with her computers to take a look. He spent his entire non-teaching time that day working on the problem, and finally retrieved the information. His willingness and expertise were invaluable.

"The real voyage of discovery consists not in seeking new landscapes but in having new eyes."   *- Marcel Proust*

I should not conclude this section with the idea that all experienced teachers struggle with technology. Our school's most skillful computer technician has over twenty-five years of teaching experience and stays current on technology issues. She is willing to help whenever she can. It takes an entire staff to create a quality school.

Professional Organizations: Professional organizations provide numerous services to their members. Phi Delta Kappa International, with over 50,000 members, deals with education issues, but does not organize to negotiate contracts. Its various services, including the periodical The Phi Delta Kappan, explore a variety of educational issues and keep members informed on the most recent research in the field. Phi Delta Kappa maintains international, national, and state chapters. The American Federation of Teachers (1.3 million members) and the National Education Association (2.8 million members) differ from Phi Delta Kappa by providing staff and services for contract negotiations, thereby acquiring the moniker "teacher unions." Both groups publish periodicals and newsletters which keep members informed on academic as well as labor-related issues. All three organizations require a fee for membership. While membership in AFT or NEA is mutually exclusive, you may join Phi Delta Kappa and either AFT or NEA. The great advantage of belonging to two professional educational organizations lies in your opportunity to assess differing perspectives on current educational trends such as the No Child Left Behind Act, charter schools, school reform, and teacher compensation. (Note: enrollment figures for all three organizations are from 2006).

You may also join professional organizations in your specialized area. For example, I have been a member of the National Council of Teachers of English. Other disciplines and other levels of instruction (elementary, middle school, and high school) have specialized professional organizations which provide information and services in more narrowly defined positions.

All of the above mentioned organizations give you the opportunity to expand your knowledge of current research, data, and trends in education and can provide you with needed support via web sites, articles, and conferences and workshops. Once you commit to a career in the classroom, consider enhancing your professional range of knowledge by joining a professional organization.

Deciding whether or not to join your local, state, and national education association is a serious decision you will make as a career teacher. Research your local association, including percentage of membership, dues, contract negotiations history, and services provided. Views vary nation wide on the role of teacher unions. Some feel that they protect the weak, do not police themselves well enough, and allow ineffective teachers to remain in the classroom at the expense of the students. Others feel that unions provide needed protection from frivolous sanctions, guarantee that teachers can negotiate their salaries and benefits with their employers, and promote the teaching profession.

The truth, in my estimation, lies somewhere in the middle. I have been a career-long member of the Dubuque Education Association, the Iowa State Education Association, and the National Education Association. I have no regrets about being a member; in fact, I am proud to be part of a large national association of professionals. I haven't always agreed with the policies of the local, state, and national bodies, but I support their efforts to sustain and enhance the quality of teaching across the nation. Nothing angers me more than to hear a nonmember say to me, "Can you believe what our bargaining team settled for? That's terrible!" I have said on more than one occasion, "Since you are not a member and pay no dues, perhaps you would like to negotiate your contract on your own. I'm sure you can do much better." That usually silences the person.

"Only the mediocre are always at their best."

- Anonymous

CRAFTING YOUR CRAFT AND
BUILDING YOUR REPUTATION

As you become more adept in the classroom through better planning, better adapting of lessons, better classroom management skills, better snap decision-making skills, and better relationships with students, your reputation will grow. Students will talk about you outside of class in a positive manner. When that happens, you will notice fewer problems; students will have certain expectations before they enter your classroom. If you work hard in your first years to build relationships, to make the classroom relevant to students' lives, and to challenge students with quality instruction, you have taken the first steps to becoming a master teacher.

How do you become respected and popular among students and still be demanding in the classroom? First, continually refine the courses you teach, enriching them with relevant allusions to students' lives. Second, borrow as much information from your colleagues as you can. Third, continually seek ways to build relationships with students of all abilities and backgrounds.

I see the classes I teach as organic rather than static. I add and delete material every semester, and I look for enriching tidbits from contemporary news sources to enhance the relevance of the lessons. For example, I teach the Stephen King short story, "Survivor Type," a gruesome tale of a narcissistic surgeon who loses his medical license and tries to raise money for his effort to regain it by smuggling heroin into the country. His ship sinks, and he's stranded on a lifeless island with no food. Within days, he must decide if he wants to starve or survive. He chooses the latter, performs surgeries on himself and cannibalizes himself. Some students think the story is too far-fetched, even for King. However, several years ago, a young man was trapped in a remote area of Utah when a boulder wedged itself between his arm and his torso. Facing starvation, the young man made a difficult decision and amputated the arm, freeing himself from the boulder and allowing him to escape and find his way to discovery. While the young man did not resort to the post-amputation nutrition option that Richard Pine did, I tell my students that this young man is a real-life example of a "Survivor Type," and I emphasize how powerful the human desire to live is in the face of a life-threatening situation. To keep your classes relevant at whatever level you teach, you must know what is happening in the world, especially events that affect the lives of your students.

> **"I not only use all the brains that I have but all that I can borrow."**
> *- Woodrow Wilson*

When I mentioned borrowing material, I meant that you can enrich your lessons, your delivery, and your assessment by talking with other teachers, and with their permission, examining their materials. In my first years of teaching, I borrowed everything I could get my hands on. I frequently discussed the lessons with the teachers who offered the lessons to me. I kept what I felt would work for me and I discarded what I felt would not work. I did this with daily lessons, quizzes, study questions, individual and group activities. I am indebted to the teachers who so willingly shared their talents. Now late in my career, I have given young teachers my folders of units to peruse from classes I once taught or classes I currently teach with them. If we are true colleagues, we will

---

"When love and skill work together, expect a masterpiece."
- John Ruskin

be flattered that younger teachers look to us for assistance, and we will realize that providing materials for teachers to use, modify, and strengthen ultimately benefits the students.

COMMUNITY INVOLVEMENT

During this phase of your career, you may explore opportunities for community involvement. Serving on advisory boards, volunteering at the local community theater, volunteering at your political party's local offices, or volunteering for a local environmental group's cleanup initiatives are ways to encounter other community members, expand your social circle, and gain more respect from members in the community, perhaps even some who are critical of the schools! You may have a chance to change some attitudes.

MONITORING AND MANAGING STRESS

With additional duties both at school and at home, it is crucial to manage the stresses in your life so that you can be effective and productive and mentally healthy. Monitor your work load, and if you have to say no to something, say no. Envision the long view of your career, and distribute your energy accordingly. I have been fortunate to make what I feel are good decisions during my career, and as I near the end, I feel as passionate and energetic as ever.

One significant recommendation I can make regarding stress management and career structuring is the importance of maintaining a reasonable level of physical fitness. I started running in my second year of teaching, and I know that my energy level and enthusiasm have remained strong because of running. There is a certain cleansing, even purging, that comes with a good bout of exercise, and I have run off many stressful encounters and formulated many lesson plans and strategies for dealing with tense situations while running. Being fit builds confidence in oneself and respect from others, provides good modeling, and can be inspirational to others. Don't allow yourself to abandon regular exercise as your career develops; it can be the most critical component in maintaining the drive for continual improvement as your career unfolds.

"The world talks to the mind. A teacher speaks more intimately; he talks to the heart."   *- Haim Ginott*

By the end of this phase of your career, you may come to a crossroads. In the movie "Teachers," a student and a teacher both experience emotional crises. The student, arriving at school after a period of absence, faces the teacher, who asks the student, "You gonna stay, or are you gonna go?" The student walks out before answering. As the movie nears its end, the teacher, a former teacher of the year, now under pressure to resign, comes into his classroom after the meeting to dismiss him and faces his students. The absentee student is there, and says to the teacher, "You gonna stay, or are you gonna go?" It's a tense moment, because both student and teacher have contemplated leaving, and it dramatizes the moments in a teacher's career when she or he faces the biggest question of all: to stay or to go. If you stay, the next ten years can become the time when you move from a thriving professional to a master teacher at the top of your profession.

CASE STUDY #18

SENSITIVE PERSONAL ISSUES

During my years as a cross country coach, I encountered a number of sensitive personal issues with the young women I coached. One Saturday morning, one of my runners, a sophomore, came to practice with a black eye. She was also upset and appeared to have been crying.

Before we started practice, I called her aside and asked her if everything was OK. She started to cry and said, "No, everything is not OK."

I asked her if she wanted to talk about it, and she told me, "My brother beat me up last night."

This young woman was a talented young runner, but she came from a challenging background. She was in a single parent home, and her brother had a history of fighting and was involved with racist peers.

I knew what action I needed to take, and I believe I did the right thing. What did I do?

- • **Call the young woman's mother and ask to talk to her?**

- • **Call the residence and ask to talk to the young woman's brother to see if the story was credible?**

- • **Tell the young woman to tell me if her brother hit her again?**

- • **Report the incident to the school nurse?**

Discussion of this case study on page 221

CASE STUDY #19

DEALING WITH A PARENT DURING THE SCHOOL DAY

In mid-September one year, I was teaching my fifth period class when our activities coordinator appeared at my door with a woman. I stopped class and went to the door. The activities coordinator introduced the woman as the mother of one of my freshmen cross country runners, then walked away. I thought she came to explain that her daughter couldn't run in the meet that day because the girl was sick or some family issue had come up.

Instead, the woman expressed concern that it was too hot that day, and her daughter might dehydrate and collapse at the race site. She wondered if I knew enough about competing and hydration.

I was dumbfounded. The high that day was barely 80 degrees, and the team had practiced in similar conditions for the past month. I explained to the woman that I had over twenty years experience in coaching cross country and was a competitive runner myself. I assured her that I would take all necessary precautions to ensure that the runners were hydrated and that I would look for signs of dehydration during the races. She finally left, still expressing some concern about the conditions that day.

After nearly five minutes, I returned to my class.

What would you do as a follow up to such a situation?

- **Thank the administrator for directing the parent to your classroom?**

- **Tell the administrator to notify you before sending parents to your room during the school day?**

- **Go to the principal and complain about the administrator's actions?**

Discussion of this case study on page 223

CASE STUDY #20

A STRUGGLING STUDENT TEACHER

You have been teaching just long enough to qualify for supervision of a student teacher. As the year begins, you and the student teacher establish a working relationship. She observes intently and asks pertinent questions about classroom management, instruction, and planning. As the date draws close for her to take over her first classes, she becomes noticeably nervous. You work with her on lesson plans every day, and cover, day by day, the first week. Two days before she takes over, you ask to see the lesson plans. She has none. She says it's really hard to think of how to fill the class period. You ask, "Are you ready to teach the class?" She responds, "I don't think so."

What do you do?

- **Make her teach? It's time to sink or swim!**

- **Contact her supervisor and ask for a conference with the three of you?**

- **Tell her it's OK and that she can start with the next unit?**

- **Agree to introduce the unit, then let her take over?**

Discussion of this case study on page 225

CASE STUDY #21

DIRECTING STUDENTS TO MORE CHALLENGING CLASSES

You supervise a computer lab which is open to all classes. One day a special education class comes in to work on an assignment on the computers. You soon notice that one student works very efficiently and accurately. She completes her assignment without asking for assistance, then helps other students who have trouble with either the computers or their assignments.

You wonder, does this student belong in this class?

I believe I handled this situation well.

What would you do?

Discussion of this case study on page 227

CASE STUDY #22

FUNDRAISERS AND REWARDS

You are a young teacher in a middle school that prides itself on providing students with field trip opportunities. In recent years, however, the school district has cut funding for such trips and placed responsibility on individual schools.

Your class is participating in a fundraiser that will subsidize a student trip to a major event in a big city. You distribute the information to your students and talk to them about the importance of raising money for the valuable educational experience.

The end of the fundraiser coincides with a major test. To reward the students who raised money, you announce that students who sold items for the fundraiser will be allowed to use their books for the test, and those who chose not to participate will not.

A student who did not raise any money objects, claiming that your decision is unfair, and says she will tell her parents.

What would you do?

- **Ignore the complaint and allow only the sellers to use their books on the test?**

- **Change the test so that sellers will have only a small advantage on it?**

- **Change your mind and allow all students to use their books?**

- **Take back the announcement and don't allow any students to use their books during the test?**

Discussion of this case study on page 229

Chapter 5:

Years Eleven through Twenty:
Internalizing Lessons, Assuming Leadership Roles
and Mentoring New Teachers

The sixth thing you must know to become a master teacher:

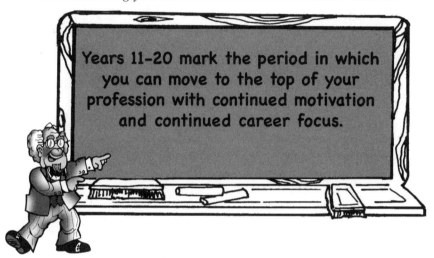

Years 11-20 mark the period in which you can move to the top of your profession with continued motivation and continued career focus.

A   s you enter the second decade of teaching, some things become easier: less preparation time, greater familiarity with student challenges, greater familiarity with the school district's policies and practices. The school year seems less fragmented; rather, it becomes more like a continuum than an abruptly shifting series of segments of intense work followed by segments of time off. If you have pursued advanced degrees or attained national certification, the coursework by this stage lessens, unless you have delayed accumulating additional hours. Yes, teaching does become a more familiar task. But it is also in these years that many teachers experience diminished drive; teaching well becomes enough. There is a fine line between comfort and complacency, and complacency is the enemy of continued growth. In this chapter, I will explore the primary issues that make the difference between becoming static or dynamic in the "middle age" of a career in the classroom:

- Maintaining a passion for instruction
- Increasing leadership roles
- Achieving recognition from students, peers, and others
- Handling the evolving demands of your personal life

MAINTAINING A PASSION FOR INSTRUCTION

Above all, persistence of passion for teaching is the defining trait of a master teacher. Master teaching is far more complex than most scholarly research reveals, because some of its features are unmeasurable. In this era of obsession with data, assessment, and outcomes, much of the current research in education places too little emphasis on the qualities of the teaching persona that motivate and inspire students to learn. In one of my lessons, I ask students to list the traits of an effective teacher. Invariably, they list such elements as sense of humor, ability to relate lessons to students' lives, ability to make learning fun (through teaching techniques), ability to maintain high expectations, and treating all students equally. They do not list such things as having the most lavish portfolio, attending the most workshops on authentic assessment, and teaching only what the curriculum dictates.

"I put the relation of a fine teacher to a student just below the relation of a mother to a son."   *- Thomas Wolfe*

If passion is so important, what is it? In my estimation...

Passion is the heart of teaching. It is the combination of physical and intellectual effort in delivering lessons in which the objective is that all students will attend and learn. It is a force, a presence, that commands attention and demands effort without stating it. Passion is the intersection of the mastery of the material, the love of the material, the desire to communicate it, and the desire for students to acquire and internalize that material. It is the transference of knowledge and the transference of mastery, and when combined with a transference of compassion, it is the greatest gift we can give to our young people.

Teachers who continue to teach with passion need not worry about growing old in their careers. They will retire as vital in their teaching as they were in their first years.

How does one retain passion after teaching for so many years? There are several factors involved. First, maintain a passion for the material you teach. Regardless of your assignment, and regardless of the number of years you've taught the material, teach it with the force and certainty and the same high expectations that you did when you first internalized it; it must never get old. Second, find new ways to make the material relevant to the lives of the students–new angles, new connections, new nuances. Keep the material alive by breathing new life into it. Third, refine the methods by which you deliver the lessons. Develop more dramatic methods of presentation, devise new activities that maximize engagement, refine your assessment methods. Fourth, maintain a physical and intellectual presence in the classroom. Continuing dedication to fitness, intellectual growth, and the capacity for wonder provide the finest modeling for the students who watch you every day.

Maintaining passion for teaching takes dedication, commitment, and diligence. What greater traits can we foster in our students than dedication, commitment, and diligence, which lead invariably to passion?

"Good teaching must be slow enough so that it is not confusing, and fast enough so that it is not boring."   *- Sidney Harris*

INCREASING LEADERSHIP ROLES

In this phase of your career, assert mastery outside of the classroom if you want others to see you as a master teacher. As your powers develop, extend into other areas. Depending on the opportunities in your school, you can assume leadership roles at both the building and district levels. Within your school, you can move from being a participant in various groups to being a leader of them. You can become a team leader, chair of the site council, department chair, mentoring coordinator, or technology mentor. At the district level, you can serve on committees which address professional development, assessment, curriculum initiatives, or long-range planning. You may even pursue leadership roles on the state and national levels through such avenues as the AFT, NEA, Phi Delta Kappa, and more specific organizations at your level. Leadership roles demand time, effort, and organization, and should never be pursued at the expense of your teaching. But the rewards–greater respect from your peers, greater connectedness with the school and district, and greater influence in the direction of your school–are significant. Weigh these benefits against the commitment of time and effort. Becoming a leader in both the classroom and in the school can be a vitalizing and enriching experience at this period of your career.

ACHIEVING RECOGNITION FROM PEERS, STUDENTS, PARENTS, AND OTHERS

If you maintain a passion for teaching, continue to learn, and develop a presence in your school, you will be rewarded. Recognition comes in many forms throughout one's career–a student saying, "I like your class"; a parent thanking you at conferences; a principal acknowledging your work; a nomination for teacher of the year; a state award; a national award. At this point in your career, these moments of recognition are affirming and sustaining. A nice compliment from a student can make your week; a teacher recognition award from a college based on a former student's recommendation can make your month; a statement from a parent that her or his child is pursuing a career in teaching because of you can make your year. No matter how competent you become, compliments feed the soul. They tell you that you are good, that you do make a difference. And when you finish a rough day when the lesson plans did not work as you wanted them to, you can reflect on those affirmations and know that tomorrow will be better.

If you receive recognition in the form of a plaque or a frameable document, display it in your classroom. Displaying plaques of recognition is not vain; it tells students that they are in a quality classroom of a teacher who has earned that recognition. You should send that message. Finally, receiving recognition bolsters the image of professionalism which our profession does not pursue with enough vigor. Share your good fortune with others.

Ms. Rose,
I really
loved your
class.
I'll keep
in touch.
      - Ryan

That's worth three teacher of the year nominations!

"A wise man learns from his mistakes, but an even wiser man learns from somebody else's mistakes."   **- T.D.R**

HANDLING THE CHANGING DEMANDS
OF YOUR PERSONAL LIFE

Years 11-20 correspond in chronological age from the early thirties to late forties. If you have children, this period can be the busiest of your life. Juggling family and career is an art, and if you are a teacher, your spouse or significant other will be employed full time as well. Children of the educators I know lead active lives outside of school, so you may be required to take your children to lessons, attend sporting events, host gatherings, organize carpools, coordinate fundraisers, supervise homework, answer cell phone calls from your children during evenings, and enforce curfews. Parenting, I tell my students, is the hardest job you will ever have: it is a twenty-four hour a day job, and it never ends. You are always on call. Maintaining a dynamic career and being an involved parent takes tremendous energy and commitment. Assess your performances in both areas to ensure you balance the demands of being a good teacher, parent, and partner. When in doubt, "family first" is a good rule.

Fortunately, in this period you are still young enough and energetic enough to handle the multitasking necessary to remain vital. As you near the end of your career and reflect, you will be amazed that you did all you did during this phase of your career. I know I get tired just thinking of the frenzied pace I led during these years, but I don't regret any of it. As Lucinda Matlock says in Edgar Lee Masters' The Spoon River Anthology, "It takes life to love life." Or, as my friend Bill Duggan says, "We're only here for a short stay." Have at it!

CASE STUDY #23

STUDENT
VS.
STUDENT ASSISTANCE

You are teaching an elective course for upper classmen. One of your students has had some problems during the semester and has missed a great deal of class. On this day near the end of the semester, the student is present and is ready to take a major test. The test is crucial; the student is near failing, and needs a good performance on this test to have a chance to pass.

Ten minutes into the test, someone delivers a pass for the student from the guidance office telling the student to come immediately to the guidance area to see a counselor from a community mental health facility.

What do you do?
Discussion of this case study on page 231

CASE STUDY #24

WORKING WITH A STUDENT TEACHER

You are an experienced teacher. You agree to supervise a student teacher for a semester. The student teacher is bright and competent, and knows the students well after only a short time. Everything is going well. The student teacher takes over several classes and creates effective lesson plans.

One day after he finishes a lesson, you remind students of some upcoming events (marking periods, parent conferences). As you talk, you notice the students smirking, smiling, and laughing. Since the material you are discussing is mundane, you quickly turn around and notice that the student teacher is mimicking you behind your back. You finish the comments, the bell rings, and the students leave.

What action do you take?

- **Teacher A thought it over, did not see it as a major issue, and let the event pass.**

- **Teacher B thought it over, formulated a response, and at the end of the day told the student teacher that what he did was inexcusable and rude. Teacher B also told the student teacher that he was considering contacting the student teacher's supervisor and requesting either a conference or a change in cooperating teachers.**

Discussion of this case study on page 233

CASE STUDY #25

CREATIVE DISCIPLINE

In around my tenth year of teaching, I felt confident in the classroom. I'd moved beyond overreacting to incidents, and I had a good rapport with my students. During the fall of the year, I was writing on the board when suddenly something hit me squarely in the back of the head. Someone in the class had thrown a hacky sack and pegged me perfectly. The students were shocked and they awaited my response. I picked up the hacky and said, "Whose hacky is this?" To my surprise, a student raised his hand and acknowledged that it was his. "Thank you, Mr. _____, I'll keep this as evidence," I said, and returned immediately to the lesson.

How do you think I responded to this incident?

Discussion of this case study on page 235

Chapter 6:

Years Twenty-One through Retirement: Managing the Third Decade and Beyond

The seventh thing you must know to become a master teacher:

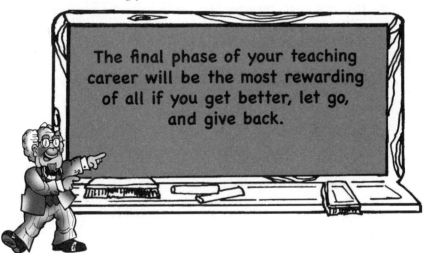

The final phase of your teaching career will be the most rewarding of all if you get better, let go, and give back.

A s I near the end of my career and I reflect on my years of teaching, I am proud of my contributions to my students, my school, and my district. I have led an active and well managed career. By monitoring my levels of performance, passion, and energy, I feel as vital and excited in my fourth decade of teaching as I did in my first decade. The key to longevity is to make the final years not years of hanging on, but years of forging ahead–of maintaining excellence in the classroom, of modeling, mentoring and guiding young teachers, and of leaving a legacy for others to follow. In this final chapter, I will discuss how to leave teaching at the top of your profession–respected, admired, and in some cases, beloved, of leaving the classroom for the last time and saying, "A job well done," rather than saying, "Thank God I survived." To reach that climactic moment, the final years must involve three crucial components:

- Continuing to improve in the classroom
- Pacing your career
- Leaving a legacy which younger teachers will carry on

"How you teach is more important than what you teach."
                                                   -Anonymous

THANK GOD I SURVIVED.

A JOB WELL DONE.

CONTINUING TO IMPROVE IN THE CLASSROOM

The most important aspect of the final years of teaching is maintaining a commanding presence in the classroom. This can be a challenge for several reasons. First, if you retain the same teaching assignment, the lessons become repetitious, and as you hear yourself telling the same stories and presenting the same material, you can find yourself losing interest in the content which so inspired you earlier in your career. To avoid this, consider the following: first, polish your anecdotal material, so it sounds fresh to you; second, develop new approaches which reflect who you are now; third, update your lessons, so that you present the content in a new way or with a new slant; fourth, request a new assignment. While the fourth option is the most radical, it may be necessary if you find yourself stagnating. I was fortunate that in my 25th year, I assumed a new assignment, an Advanced Placement class, which demanded an enormous amount of work, but which also revitalized my career. I consider myself lucky to have had that opportunity.

"*Any teacher that can be replaced by a computer should be replaced by a computer.*"

-Anonymous

Working with younger colleagues can be refreshing, too. Often younger professionals have the benefit of the most recent educational information regarding methods, infusion of technology, lesson design and delivery, and assessment. My experiences with mentoring new teachers enable me to revise my own teaching repertoire. Inservice and CEU requirements may not provide the depth of study or degree of relevance to inspire changes which make a qualitative difference in your teaching persona. Mine the young; they may be your mentors in the final years–a nice thought.

The most important thing to remember about remaining vibrant in the classroom is that students expect you to be good. Don't let them down. Their brothers and sisters, their aunts and uncles, and in some cases, their mothers and fathers have touted you as a "must have" teacher. If your reputation precedes you, live up to it until the day you retire.

I have done some quirky things to keep myself vibrant in the classroom. In recent years, I developed a personal challenge to collect papers as rapidly as possible. I position myself near the first desk, set my watch, and sprint through the two rows of the semicircle, gathering papers hand-over-hand, and stop the watch when I collect the last paper. My fastest time is 11.26 seconds for twenty-eight papers. Students love watching me do it. This atypical behavior serves three significant purposes: one, it saves class time; two, students see that I still have a lot of energy–I am still quick on my feet and my hand-eye coordination is still sharp; third, I'm still a little "weird." Why not give them something to talk about outside of the class?

PACING YOUR CAREER

In the final years of your career, assess how much work you can handle outside of the classroom. Some activity sponsors relish their duties for their entire careers. Two perfect examples occurred in my school. First, our men's track and field coaching staff, consisting of four full-time teachers, recently completed twenty five successful years of coaching together. Another teacher retired a few years ago after teaching speech and sponsoring our award-winning speech and theater programs for thirty-three years. Today, our auditorium is named for her.

The above examples are inspirational and certainly not isolated. While coaching or sponsoring activities such as theater, debate, and student council provides meaningful interactions with students, they also involve dealing with students failing to follow through, students quitting, parents questioning your decisions, teachers complaining about students being away from class, administrators demanding accountability and success, and your own desire and drive. Honestly assess your enthusiasm for such extra duties. If you love the involvement and the students respond to your leadership, there is no reason to retire from co-curricular sponsorship. However, once you find that the negative aspects of activity sponsorship outweigh the positive ones, it is time to let someone else do the job. One of the great mistakes excellent teachers and activity sponsors make late in their careers is not letting go, rationalizing with such thoughts as, "The students need me," or "No one can do the job I'm doing," or "I'd like to finish my career when these students graduate." These are all noble but questionable reasons for continuing. One of my colleagues and best

---

"A great memory does not make a mind any more than a dictionary is a piece of literature." **- John Henry Newman**

friends likes to cite the saying, "The cemeteries are filled with indispensable people." I know that when I retired from coaching after twenty-eight years, I missed the contact I had with the students, but I didn't miss the bus rides and the attendant late nights and early mornings. Unless activity sponsorship is your passion, know when enough is enough.

"The second most important job in the world, second only to being a good parent, is being a good teacher." — S.G. Ellis

LEAVING A LEGACY

If you have led a productive, vibrant, and exemplary career in the classroom, it is imperative that you share your cumulative knowledge with those who will follow you. When our school's Advanced Placement teacher retired and I took over his classes, I asked him for help with lesson plans and materials. He told me that he was writing a book and that he could not share his materials with me for that reason. I was shocked and quite concerned. How would I teach these capable students without any mentoring? Fortunately, I attended a week-long workshop the summer before I taught the class and I read the major works and studied them so that I would be prepared. My first year was a challenge: I worked hard and my students performed well on the national exam, but it was an unnecessarily stressful year. Whoever teaches the class after I retire will have all the resources I have amassed in the years I have taught it. It is unconscionable for a master teacher to withhold his or her wisdom and materials from the teacher who assumes the teaching assignment.

Note: I await the release of the book, nine years after I took over the class.

What, then, does a capable, experienced, successful teacher do to ensure that those who follow in her/his footsteps begin with support, both academically and emotionally? Three words form the answer to that question:

- Mentoring (formal and informal)
- Modeling
- Maintaining

Formal Mentoring: Mentoring can occur on both formal and informal bases. Being a formal mentor means that you participate in your district's structured mentoring program, which assigns you to a specific new teacher. One of the best ways to avoid becoming cynical and negative near the end of your career is to mentor. Working with a new teacher will take you back to your own beginnings. As you see yourself in the new teacher, you realize the tremendous effort you have expended to reach the level of respect, maturity, and admiration you have earned, and you want the new teacher to take the journey, too. Sometimes a navigator, sometimes a guide, sometimes a copilot, the more you reflect on this relationship, the more you will take pride in your career. Making the way a little easier for a new teacher makes your final steps a little easier, too.

"A mind is a fire to be kindled, not a vessel to be filled."
- Plutarch

Informal Mentoring: Informal mentoring involves working with a new teacher primarily in curriculum areas. It does not delve as deeply into the professional issues as a formal mentoring relationship, but it can be a tremendous experience. It does not include required components of formal mentoring, and it can end any time. Whether it is a course alike or grade alike situation, experienced teachers can model the nuances of planning lessons, delivering them, and evaluating them. For overwhelmed new teachers, this relationship can save valuable time, and permanently influence the content and style of the new teacher's material and persona. For those experienced teachers who do not want the added responsibility of an assigned new teacher through formal mentoring, informal mentoring is a way to share knowledge and wisdom that can strengthen the instructors and instruction in your building.

Modeling: If you want to finish your career quietly by teaching your classes and avoiding any extra responsibilities, that is fine. After over thirty years, you deserve to slow the pace and leave the extra stuff to younger staff who have more invested in the future of the school. Modeling professional and compassionate teaching can be a great gift. One of my experienced colleagues continues to assert himself in our building without performing extra duties. One of my students told me that when school started in the fall, she was ill and missed the first two weeks of school. She thought of dropping out, but got a letter from my colleague saying he hoped she would recover quickly and get back to school and that he'd adjust her work load to allow her to gradually catch up. She said she wouldn't have come back if she hadn't received that letter. He composes poetry for special occasions such as retirements and weddings, earning the facetious title "Poet Lariat" of our school. Every year at the homecoming assembly he sings a rousing song he composed which inspires the students. Without great fanfare, he touches many in our building by playing to his strengths–creativity and compassion. Another of my colleagues who is incredibly well-organized works with one of our young teachers who struggles with organization. Quietly, she's making a difference for the young teacher.

As you near the end of your career, channeling your strengths can have significant effects on staff and students. Know what you do well and keep doing it!

Share your talents.

"The length of your education is less important than its breadth, and the length of your life is less important than its depth."
- Marilyn Vos Savant

Maintaining: In recent years, changes in technology, changes in state and federal legislation, and changes in the public's perception of education have made teaching a more complex profession. The older we get as teachers, the more difficult it is to smoothly adjust to these changes. Waxing nostalgic, "In my day..." has limited benefits. It usually prefaces a complaint. It is important to deal with these changes near the end of your career. Being obstructionist and negative can overshadow legitimate concerns about some of the changes in education. The voices of experience are necessary to balance the voices of impetuosity. Make sure the voices of experience are heard clearly. There are few things in education that are more disheartening than a teacher who retires with a bitter heart and a sour attitude. Effort and struggle define a career in the classroom. To see that effort and struggle end in acrimony and resentment diminishes the profession. Above all, maintain your energy and presence in the classroom. Your students can be your saving grace. They need you to teach and guide them. Keep them in focus. I will always remember Christa McAuliffe's simple but profound statement, "I touch the future. I teach."

If you struggle at the end of your career, work at maintaining a strong presence in the classroom, and share your concerns with a select few–a confidant, a trusted administrator, or a mental health professional. I have seen too many excellent teachers retire at the lowest points of their careers. A colleague and good friend ended this way, and when he retired, I vowed that I would never finish my career like that. The end of one's career can be a struggle to the finish; for the sake of your profession, your students, and yourself, take the last steps toward retirement as firmly and resolutely as you can.

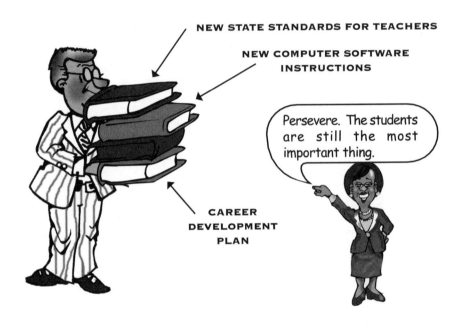

"I was only a little mass of possibilities. It was my teacher (Anne Sullivan) who unfolded and developed them....She never since let pass an opportunity to make my life sweet and useful."   *- Helen Keller*

As you count down the final days, I hope you look back and see years of continual improvement, reflection, adjustment, and enthusiasm. I hope you reflect on the thousands of lives you touched, guided, and inspired. When you walk out of the classroom for the last time, I hope that you leave your school knowing that you made it a better place, that you gave your heart, mind, and soul to teaching, and that you retire at the happiest moment of your career.

"A child's mind is like a shallow brook with ripples and dances merrily over the stonily course of its education and reflects here a flower, there a bush, yonder a fleecy cloud . . ."   - Helen Keller

CASE STUDY #26

WHEN A MENTOR FAILS

You are a seasoned veteran. As a natural progression to your career, you become involved in your district's mentoring program for new teachers. You receive training to mentor new teachers, you receive further training to train teachers to mentor new teachers, and you are your building's leader in mentoring issues. Each year you mentor a new teacher, train twenty to forty teachers to become mentors, and you work with the principal to place mentors with new teachers in your building.

Near the end of the first semester, a new teacher approaches you with some disturbing news. His mentor has failed to establish contact with him and they do not meet on a regular basis. Even after he asked the mentor to meet to discuss some challenges he was facing, the mentor did not follow through, canceling several meetings and not showing up for an after-school meeting.

With a semester of neglect (mentoring is a paid position) against him, it is obvious that the mentor is not performing satisfactorily.

What do you do?

Discussion of this case study on page 237

CASE STUDY #27

HELPING A NEW TEACHER

You are an experienced, well-respected teacher. One day while you research an upcoming unit in the main learning center, a group of twenty students noisily comes in and sits down at six tables near you. They continue to talk when they sit down, and the learning center supervisor has to ask them to be quiet.

After two more minutes, the teacher, in his second year, arrives and gives the students general instructions about the research assignment. The students, already engaged in conversation, pay little attention, and are slow to begin the task. One student has a question, and the teacher goes to the student's table to help, turning his back on the rest of the class. The chatter continues. At the table nearest you, four young women make small talk. One checks her makeup. Another checks for messages on her cell phone. Since you can't get any work done, you glance at the other tables and notice little engagement.

The learning center supervisor approaches the area, obviously upset. You leave, unable to get any work done.

What do you do in this situation?

- **Let the teacher and the learning center supervisor work it out?**

- **Intervene and tell the students to quiet down and get to work?**

- **Talk to the teacher about the matter?**

- **Tell the principal about the incident?**

- **If you were to talk to the teacher, what would you tell him/her?**

Discussion of this case study on page 239

Chapter 7:

Rewards and Reflections
From a Career in the Classroom

The following pages document various stages of my career. They include speeches and writings ranging from graduation speeches to cross country season summaries to comments from parents, colleagues, and former students to recognition from institutions of higher learning.

I use these entries to demonstrate that I have built a career on both my commitment to continuing professional development and my commitment to my students.

Because teachers thrive on compliments, I have also included several I have received from students, colleagues, administrators, and parents. I hope they provide a glimpse of the rewards of a teaching career.

MY 2004 GRADUATION SPEECH

I've lost count of the number of times I've spoken at our school's graduation ceremonies. I selected this speech because it focuses on what students taught me rather then what I taught them.
One note, Dan Klavitter, is disabled: His legs are abnormally short and he must use a wheel chair. Dan refused to accept his disability as an impediment to athletic achievement.

Platform guests, graduates, students, parents, and friends,

I am honored that you selected me to speak at tonight's graduation ceremonies. Thank you for the opportunity. I am also honored to speak with Mr. Mitchell, who has been my principal for 18 years. Thank you, Mr. Mitchell for your leadership, your stewardship, and your confidence in the staff at Senior.

As I contemplated this speech, I thought to myself, "Thirty-five years after graduating from high school, what advice can I give these graduates that could make a difference?" Then I asked myself another question: "What have you students taught me this year?" After some reflection, I thought of three examples of your behaviors that enriched my life this year and that I think can make a difference in your lives after you walk out of this building: having a sense of humor, having someone to inspire you, and having a life-long commitment to being the best person you can be.

April Meyer told me to make my speech humorous. That was good advice. Being able to laugh is not only good for the soul, it is good for the body. I have found humor, in appropriate forms, is a key to happiness. And being able to laugh at ourselves is a key to humor. For example, during second semester in third period Contemporary Lit.—Amber Waddick, Cassie Tater, Steve

---

"In a completely rational society, the best of us would be teachers and the rest of us would have to settle for something less, because passing civilizations along from one generation to the next ought to be the highest honor and the highest responsibility anyone could have." - Lee Iacocca

Adams, and Ed Beecher are witnesses—I got up to put some-thing in the recycling bin and tripped over the corner of my open desk drawer, landing flat on my back. While the students I men-tioned burst into what I thought was sadistic laughter, I made a quick check to see if I was injured and sensing I wasn't, muttered, "Very funny, I'm dying of laughter down here," which inspired them to even more laughter. Sometimes we just have to laugh, even if it is at our own expense. Thank you for reminding me of the importance of humor.

On a more serious note, role models are hard to come by these days, if we impose the standards of celebrity and fame onto the definition. I prefer to choose those who achieve quietly and con-sistently over time, and I particularly admire those who over-come adversity. This year my inspiration was Danny Klavitter. Dan, as you may know, finished second in the state wrestling tournament at 103 pounds. He was tough and focused, but that is not what impressed me the most. Dan's dedication in the off-season made me admire his achievements. In the fall the cross country team uses the wrestling room to meet and stretch. From early September, two months before the wrestling season, Dan would be there when we left, working out on his own, preparing for the season. So when he accepted his second place medal at the state meet in February, and I saw the disappointment on his face, my admiration only grew. Despite overcoming great ob-stacles, Dan was not satisfied. Despite the challenges he faced, he aspired for perfection. I will never forget that.

I have a small poster in my classroom that reads, "Doing your best means never stop trying." I'll let you graduates in on a little secret: those inspirational posters that many of us teachers have plastered on our walls are as much for us as they are for you. As a teacher, I know that I am only as good as the last class I have taught. I have long lived by the idea that excellence is a daily pursuit, and that excellence and persistence go hand in hand. It's not always easy to stay on task. This year, Lucas Gonyier demonstrated the qualities of improvement and achievement at a level I have rarely witnessed. Last year, Lucas was in my Basic Lit class and did remarkably well. I encouraged him to take Contemporary Lit., a definite step up. Lucas aced Contemporary Lit. as well, and now plans to continue his education. I am impressed with his rapid improvement, the high quality of his work, and the high standards he set for himself. His remarkable improvement inspires me to continue to evolve as a teacher.

In his poem "Theme for English B," Langston Hughes' speaker writes passionately for his class and professor about who he is, being the only African American in the class at Columbia University. He writes, "As I learn from you, I guess you learn from me." It's only fitting tonight that in the end, you have become my teachers. It is also a mark of your readiness for the next step along the path of life, and is a beautiful example of the power of education—when learners teach and teachers learn. Thank you, Class of 2004, for helping me to continue my education at Senior High. Congratulations to all of you and your families.

"They say children are the future, but really teachers are the key to the future."   **- Author unknown**

NATIONAL HONOR SOCIETY INDUCTION SPEECH 5-5-06

In addition to graduation speeches, I have also spoken at National Honor Society Inductions on three occasions. Below you will find my most recent speech and two kind responses from parents.

Ms. Swift, Mr. Anderson, Parents, Friends and NHS Inductees,

I congratulate you on your induction into National Honor Society this evening. I will direct my remarks tonight to the role you play in our school, and how I interpret the qualities of character, service, scholarship and leadership. Now, perhaps more than at any time in our school's rich history, it is imperative that you fulfill your responsibilities to NHS.

In the area of character, I challenge you to be role models in our school. I am alarmed at the number of our fine students who did not qualify for awards this year because of code of conduct violations. These misadventures reflect poorly on Senior High. Many of these violations are the result of poor judgment and immaturity. They have no place in the echelons of leadership. Demonstrate greater self-respect and self-control as NHS members. Make a commitment to character.

Our culture is far too interested in self-gratification and self-aggrandizement. Ask yourselves, what have you done for others? How have you shared your talent? How have you made Senior, and Dubuque, a better place? I ask these questions rhetorically to challenge you to give of yourselves, not to pad your resume, but to genuinely help others. Do not mistake lip service for service. Find joy in giving of yourselves rather than giving to yourselves. Discover the joy of selflessness through service.

This year marked the first year in memory that Senior High School did not have a merit scholar. We can do better than that.

If you want to truly excel, you must distinguish between being a student and being a scholar. Being a student means you take classes; being a scholar means you actively engage in learning, seeking enrichment either through questioning your teachers or pursuing knowledge for its own sake. As NHS members you cannot be casual learners; you must be models of intellectual curiosity.

Finally, you must be leaders. With our diverse population, you must exert your influence in our school. Others should look up to you; you should not look down on them. You should be examples of achievement, effort, humility, and pride. You should be the students who bring recognition and respect to Senior. You must accept this challenge and you must not fail.

I have been assertive tonight. Rather than lavish praise on you, I exhort you to be beacons for the excellence of Senior High School. Demonstrate that NHS is not a social club, but a society committed to character, service, leadership, and scholarship. Begin that commitment tonight.

Again, congratulations to you all.

"Teaching provides a way to stay young at heart, to maintain a lifetime of active learning.....It is in every respect a profession of hope."   **- Vito Perrone**

Since April, 2006, I have contributed one column a month, entitled, "After (School) Thoughts," to the local newspaper, the Telegraph Herald. This column appeared in October of 2006. It captures the importance of establishing positive relationships with all students, and being willing to go outside of the school setting to see students from a different perspective.

TELEGRAPH TH HERALD

October 16, 2006

POETRY THAT LIVES IN STUDENT
LYRICIST BROUGHT TO THE FRONT

A Little feedback can have a positive effect

In late September, I attended a heavy metal show at the Busted Lift to see some former students, now seniors, who are in a band and who told me about the show. I was out of place not only because of my age, but also because I didn't have time to change after school and amid studded belts and body piercings, my dress shirt and tie were particularly incongruous.

My former students played first and demonstrated surprising cohesiveness, combining echoes of Metallica and Black Sabbath into their original compositions. After their set, I complimented them on their performances, and told the lead singer, Zach Gerlach, that I'd like to see the lyrics of his songs, since it was impossible to discern them over the torrent of guitar and drums. He told me that we'd connect at school.

The next day I met Zach in the hall before my prep period and he said he was ready to share the lyrics. I told him we should go to the school's library and that he should get the lyrics and meet me there. He said, "I've got them in my head." I got a legal pad and a pen and we went to a quiet corner of the library.

He took the legal pad and for the next twenty minutes wrote the lyrics to four songs. He was focused and passionate as he wrote; I could sense his energy. I was astounded. He is not among our finest students, but there he sat, spontaneously generating four lyric poems. When he finished, he turned the legal pad to me and said, "Tell me what you think, and tell me if I can improve any of it."

The first two lines of the first poem reveal his sense for the written word: "So let's set out to sea/On a journey that's already failed." His lines express immediate ironic reversal of the journey motif. Rather than center on the hopeful beginning of a journey, these lines reveal futility and failure. The poem sustains the conceit, closing with the speaker's ultimate revelation about why the journey fails: "Because you are what you've always wanted/And never was it me."

Another poem opened with the following stanza: "I take this knife to my chest/To show you how

---

"Good teachers are usually a little crazy."

- Andy Rooney

I feel about this/And how much you don't care/ I'll stand up here and share/Everything I've got/Right where X marks the spot/And spill emotion all over the stage." The violent image of the knife in the first line transforms to a microphone at the end, a symbolic representation of the pain of singing the song.

We discussed his lyrics and I offered a few suggestions on diction and imagery. When the bell rang to end school we parted, and I felt an incredible sense of exhilaration. I was honored that he would share his lyrics with me, I was impressed with his creative energy and I was dumbfounded that a student who will never take an Advanced Placement English class could compose with such spontaneity and passion.

Experiences like these make me realize why I am still in the classroom after thirty-two years.

I wrote the following piece in the summer of 1989 during a three-week course sponsored by the Iowa Writers' Project. It reflects the commitment coaches make, the stress it can create on a coach's life, and the unexpected rewards of working with young people.

FOUR BY FOUR

During the past school year I grew weary of my coaching duties. For fourteen years, I coached two sports while raising a family, maintaining a good relationship with my wife, and developing professionally as an English teacher. With the added duties as department chair the last three years, I was inching toward overload. As track season neared in February, I dreamed of divesting myself of my assistant coaching position in track at the end of the season and living a less hectic lifestyle. The more I dreamed, the more certain I became that I would resign from coaching track. I felt relieved, thinking I was doing the right thing for my students, my family, my department, and myself.

I felt this way until the state track meet in May.

It was a long season. Our head coach was distracted during the season by two things: one, his wife was expecting; two, he was appointed head football coach for the following fall. Our girls' basketball team advanced to the state tournament, which delayed the start of the season for many of our best athletes. Several of our key performers suffered injuries, which forced us to readjust our goals for the season. Despite these challenges, we had a successful season, and qualified twelve girls for the State Meet, our largest contingent in school history.

Three days before the State Meet, the head coach and his wife had their child. The timing couldn't have been worse for me. As the primary assistant, I was now in charge of the team for

---

"It is a glorious fever, that desire to know."

- Edward Lytton

the State Meet. How ironic, I thought. Here I am, eager to resign from track, now suddenly the head coach, a responsibility I did not want. I dreaded being in charge of the money, the ticket arrangements, the bed checks, and the coaching. I consoled myself by promising that this was my last duty as a track coach.

The State Meet was frustrating in some respects and disappointing in some respects. Several of our relay teams went into the meet ranked in the top six, but faltered in the preliminaries and failed to make the finals in their events. Our discus thrower, seeded second going into the meet, finished, fifth. By Saturday afternoon, as the meet drew to a close on the warm and sundrenched Jim Duncan track at Drake Stadium in Des Moines, Iowa, I thought of home and summer more than I thought of the final event of the day, the 4X400 meter relay, for which our team qualified eighth, the last qualifying team. Several of our runners suffered disappointments that day, and with our team not in contention for the overall team title, I was resigned to a seventh or eighth place finish. I would congratulate them on a great season, not say much about the race, and exit the stadium quickly for the two hundred mile trip to Dubuque.

As I sat with my stopwatch in the sun on the backstretch before the race, I reflected on each of the four runners' situations going into the race. I had no reason to hope for a good finish. Not one of them would likely be mentally or physically focused.

Our leadoff runner, Marcy, should have been the most disappointed. She qualified in three events, and failed to score in the first two. She had run four 400s in the last twenty-four hours, and had nothing to show for them. On Friday, she anchored our sprint medley team which failed to qualify for the finals. On Saturday morning, she ran brilliantly in the 4X400 preliminaries, hoping the team would break the school record in the event, knowing that by the afternoon the team would be too tired to go for the record. We missed the record by eight tenths of a second. Early Saturday afternoon, Marcy finished eighth and last in the open 400-meter dash after qualifying sixth in the preliminaries. I knew she was tired and disappointed. Her chance to be on our school's record board, her major goal as a senior, was gone. I felt sorry that she even had to run.

Sue, our second runner, was also dealing with disappointment. She recorded the slowest split in the 4X400 preliminaries Saturday morning, although not by much, but she felt partially responsible for out team's failure to break the school record. Ironically, Sue sacrificed an opportunity to break a school record to run on the 4X400 team. She was within four seconds of our school's 1500-meter record prior to the district meet, but she chose to run the 4X400 in the district meet to give the team a chance to break the school record. The 1500 is run just two races before the 4X400, so while Sue finished her warm up for the 4X400 that afternoon, she watched the 1500, and her chance for an individual school record, go by.

Anna was our third runner. The only junior among three seniors, she was the most unpredictable. Anna was also going to a prom that night at one of our city's other high schools. By qualifying for the finals in the 4X400 Anna was assured of being late for the big night. I was certain she was more eager to get home than I was.

Our anchor runner, Ana, probably had no business running the race. Her athletic career in high school was marred by a series of leg injuries, including three stress fractures. She had not run a full workout with our team since April, and had been limited to one or two races per meet. She had already run two 400s that day, and I could not imagine that she would run a third quality race with little conditioning and bad legs.

As I cleared my stopwatch and prepared to time the runners, I was sad. I didn't want the seniors' final race to be disappointing, but nothing led me to believe that it wouldn't be.

The race began. Marcy ran a controlled first half of her race, as she always does. On the final straightaway, she accelerated, finished strongly, and passed the baton to Sue. I couldn't tell what place we were in because the first runners begin with a

---

"The most beautiful thing in the world is, precisely, the conjunction of learning and inspiration. Oh, the joy of discovery!"
- Wanda Landowska

staggered start and make the first exchange at different points on the track. As she rounded the first curve and prepared to cut in to the inner portion of the track, I realized that Marcy had run a marvelous leadoff leg. Sue was in the lead pack. As the runners came by me on the backstretch, Sue lost a little ground to the four runners with her. I yelled something to Sue, something about its being her last race and not giving in. On the final curve she closed the gap on the four in front of her, and in the last 70 meters on the straightaway passed three of them with a tremendous effort. When she handed off the baton to Anna, we were in second place.

Anna, in just her first year of running the 400, was still learning how to run the race. She ran conservatively in the first 150 meters of her leg, and three runners stormed past her. I issued another exhortation, this one about not letting the others down, and hoped that she could hold on. On the final straightaway, she exploded by all three runners who had passed her and, still accelerating, passed the baton to Ana. We had regained second place.

Indianola opened an insurmountable lead and were assured of winning. Ana, tall, graceful, and determined, ran strongly. The Ames runner, the state's best overall sprinter, passed Ana at the 150 meter mark, but Ana followed her closely, knowing that even though the girl would continue to pull away, she could pull Ana away from the rest of the pack. She did. Indianola won, Ames finished second, and Ana carried us to third.

As I ran across the field to congratulate the girls, I had tears in my eyes. I didn't know what their individual times were, I didn't know what the team's total time was, but I didn't care. Time meant nothing. In four thrilling minutes, those four young women turned disappointment, injury, frustration and fatigue into a joyous conclusion to their season. When I got to them, they were embracing each other, laughing and crying. I didn't interrupt them. It was their moment. As I watched them, I was tremendously proud. As a unit, it was a collective triumph of spirit over adversity.

I will never forget it.

I did coach the next year, and for ten more years.

Teachers thrive on compliments from students, colleagues, administrators, and parents. The following entries span that range, and I hope provide a glimpse of the rewards of a teaching career.

Greetings O hypervian wanderer,

I am sure you get lots of e-mails from former students, so I will keep this short and to the point. I thought of you today because my twenty (20!) year reunion is coming up in Dubuque this year, but I doubt I will be able to attend. Still I was curious to see if you are still teaching, and am delighted to learn you are on the website roster. This is ███████████ -- remember me? I am the guy who hit you in the back of the head with a hacky-sack, and then you pulled a prank on me with Mr. Mitchell (of all people) fooling me into thinking I had done serious damage. You got me for sure! I will never forget it, nor will I forget your classes or your teaching style. In fact of my four years of high school teachers, you (along with Robert Gomoll) are the ones who made the most impact. Literature and writing have been such a large part of my life since then that I have made writing a part-time vocation, publishing under a pen name I shall not divulge. I have read many, many books since then as well - always with a critical eye towards the style, vocabulary and motif of the author. It has been a pleasure and I thank you! If you have time to write back or recommend further readings, I would love to hear from you. If my plans change about the reunion, I will let you know and perhaps we may have coffee or tea together if time allows.

Sincerely and gratefully,

███████████████████████████████

p.s. In case you are curious, I am married with three wonderful children ages 7,5 and 3. If you want to know their names, you will have to write back. Otherwise I work as a manager for a large, well-known corporation when I am not writing and having fun playing hockey and attending music festivals.

Make a wonderful day happen!:)

See case study #25 and commentary
if you think I made this up!

In February 2008 I received this email from our district Human Resources Director. I responded immediately telling him, "You made my day."

Dennis -

I was recently at a job fair where I met two aspiring English teachers. When I asked them why they were pursuing careers in education and specifically high school English, they both responded that it was because they had been inspired by having you as a teacher. Thought you might want to know.

Stan

"Anyone who stops learning is old, whether at twenty or eighty. Anyone who keeps learning stays young."   *- Henry Ford*

Carolyn Sinsky is the finest student/athlete I have taught and coached. When she was selected as a Presidential Scholar, she chose me to accompany her to Washington, D.C., for the week of recognition.

Dear Mr. Healy,

After four years as my teacher, coach, mentor, and absolute best inspiration, I can't even begin to tell you how grateful I am. You have given me direction, dreams, and energy. You have believed in me, always, and I can never forget it, because you have so strongly shaped me as a runner, a writer, and a human being. Thank you for everything. I owe who I am and where I go to you.

Carolyn

Parents become partners in education when they work with their children and their teachers, and they become even more meaningful when they acknowledge teachers' efforts. Here are two examples of appreciative parents.

Mr. Healy,

Thank you so very much for recognizing Ryan in your Commencement Speech. I was not expecting to hear his name. He just beamed when I asked him about it after graduation. Although he may not have graduated at the top of his class, he did graduate despite his struggles through school. And it's teachers like yourself who inspire students like Ryan and encourage them to do their very best. You were in a sense his mentor and he thinks very highly of you. He ▮▮▮▮ mentioned you in a class paper for NICC as a teacher who made a difference in his life. And I'm sure in all of your years there at Senior you have made a difference in a lot of students lifes! Your style of teaching is a great one! I know it motivated Ryan. Keep up the great work! Enjoy your summer. I'm sure Ryan ▮▮▮▮ will keep in touch with you! Sincerely

▮▮▮▮▮▮▮▮▮▮▮▮▮▮

"Learning is at its best when it is deadly serious and very playful at the same time."
                                                      - Sarah Lawrence Lightfoot

I taught Dave Mills and ran with him during the summers to help him prepare for cross country. This letter is from 1986.

Mr. Dennis Healy
686 West 8th
Dubuque, IA 52001

Dear Dennis:

We want you to know that the support and advice and especially
the friendship you offered Dave over the past four years has
been greatly valued by each of us.

When an excellent teacher also serves as a fine role model,
then the student is a double winner. Thanks Dennis.

Sincerely,

Carol & Gordy Mills

cc: D. Kolsrud

Aisha Isaak's father was a visiting professor at Wartburg Theological Seminary. She was a delightful and appreciative student.

Dear Mr. Healy,

"More grows in the garden than the gardener knows he has sown." This is a famous Spanish proverb that I feel, perfectly epitomizes the impression and influence, you, Mr. Healy, have left on me as well as your previous students.

I walked into your class on the 17th January, 2006, not knowing what to expect. I was informed that you were a rather "eccentric" character, much like the ones we read about throughout the semester. Not that you're a sociopathic killer ... Or at least I hope not.

I looked forward to a new semester, and a new class that would be both interesting and entertaining, two concepts that seldom come together in the class environment. I found both these things in your class. I felt at home.

Apart from the endless laughs you provided, the most important thing you did for me was believe in me. The encouragement you gave me has extended beyond the walls of Senior High. Thank you very much.

I wrote an essay on "greatness" and how desperately I'd like to achieve it. You encouraged that in me and for that, I am grateful.

"The job of a good teacher is to teach students the vitality in themselves." Joseph Campbell, a noted writer and professor once spoke these words. (I had to google him to find that out.)

"Our teachers, the best ones, did they not love what they did? Was it not their love that made us feel we wanted more? Their love made learning come alive."
- Wayne Muller

As I conclude, I'd just like to say that you have fulfilled Mr. Campbell's idea of what a good teacher is, and although it may feel difficult sometimes getting through to "Holden" like teenagers, you, Mr. Healy, have gotten through to me.

That one little comment you made to me about my writing being "excellent" meant all the world to me. That one comment has inspired me to apply that excellence in all aspects of my life. I left your class today, on the 5th of May, 2006, feeling inspired.

Thank you,
Aisha Isaak

P.S. You should come to Namibia one day, you'd enjoy it!!

I mentored Brett Bildstein during the 2006-7 school year. I taught with Brett's mother, Corlas, for a number of years, and Brett's father is also a career teacher in Dubuque. It was a pleasure to work with Brett. In two years, Brett developed rapidly in classroom management and delivery of instruction. He took a position in Chicago for the 2007-8 school year, but I hope he returns to Senior. He's good for the school. Brett and I continue to stay in touch.

As a new teacher at Senior High School, Dennis Healy became an exceptional mentor to me. I gained an infinite amount of wisdom from him through discussions and observations. I quickly noticed that although Dennis was a seasoned veteran, he never stopped searching for ways to become a better teacher. Dennis taught me the importance of connecting with students and the need for a purpose in lesson planning. Dennis was successful in balancing teaching, coaching, and family, while furthering his education. While observing Dennis teach, I realized that it is possible for a teacher to be demanding, respected, and engaging. I feel honored to call Dennis my mentor, colleague, and friend.

"Most of us end up with no more than five or six people who remember us. Teachers have thousands of people who remember them for the rest of their lives."   *- Andy Rooney*

Paul Kilgore is one of my most cherished colleagues. As he relates, I taught him and mentored him. He is a fine person and a great teacher.

I took Dennis' Contemporary Literature course as a high school junior. His enthusiasm made me want to learn and, perhaps more importantly, want to teach. Years later, as my mentor, Dennis played an important role in molding me as a young teacher. I am now in my eighth year of teaching and teach Contemporary Literature. Getting to work closely with Dennis and collaborating on the direction of this course have been perhaps the most rewarding experiences I've had as a teacher.

Elly Glass (now Elizabeth Hinders) was the finest runner I coached in my 28-year coaching career. She is one of few cross country runners in Iowa history to finish in the top ten in the State Meet all four years of high school. She graduated from Dubuque Senior in 2000, and we stay in contact. When she's in town, we run together and catch up on our lives. It's enriching to watch former student/athletes grow into adulthood. Elly competed in track and cross country at the University of Northern Iowa for four years, and recently married.

> Heals has taught me about literature, running, and most of all life. He has made such a positive impact on my life as a student and as a person. He has the ability to make anything he talks about interesting. Whenever we get together (usually runs) I always want to hear more about what he is saying, and there just never seems to be enough time. Heals makes learning enjoyable and useful. He uses his vast knowledge to share with other people. He truly is one of the most amazing people I have ever met. He not only has been my favorite teacher/coach, he has become my friend.
>
> *Elly Hinders*

"Teaching is the most responsible, the least advertised, and the worst paid, and the most richly rewarded profession in the world."
- Ian Hay

Louis Fischer is a Dubuque Senior High School graduate who graduated from Luther College in Decorah, Iowa, and now teaches at his former high school. Louis observed me during a J term, and I stayed in touch with him when he student taught and when he interviewed for jobs. Senior is fortunate to have him as a teacher and coach. He is an outstanding young educator with boundless energy, a great sense of humor, and a commanding classroom presence.

On becoming acquainted with the profession:

Some of my first experiences in the classroom occurred when I was placed under Dennis Healy's tutelage for my initial observation and practicum courses. As an observer in Dennis's classes, I was given the opportunity to view the daily workings of a high school English classroom. As those initial observations in Mr. Healy's class became more tangible as formal reflections sent to my college education professors, I recall how inspired I was by Mr. Healy's passion and dedication to his craft.

For the month I spent with Mr. Healy's classes, many responses traveled from Dubuque to Decorah relating daily lessons filled with energetic and engaging discussions between teacher and students. From Advanced Placement English discussions on the poetry of William Wordsworth to the remedial literature class's study of the tragic connections between the lives of Joplin, Presley, and Belushi, I observed students from all backgrounds and all ability levels invested and engaged in their learning. Very early on in my career as an educator, Dennis Healy became the epitome of an effective and truly meaningful educator. During our many conversations on the craft of effective teaching, we discussed classroom management and organization, professional development, and myriad other education-related topics. Looking back on those conversations, I remember most one piece of advice from Dennis that I employ on a daily basis as I plan my lessons and teach my classes: always reflect on what you are doing in your classroom. No doubt a powerful piece of advice for any young educator looking for a way to navigate through the pitfalls of those "do or die" first days in front of a class of teenagers.

Although Mr. Healy's advice on daily professional reflection was advice received early on in my teaching career, thankfully it has not been the last. For the past four years, I have had the honor of teaching next door to my mentor.

DUBUQUE SENIOR
H I G H S C H O O L

1800 Clarke Drive
Dubuque, Iowa 52001
March 17, 2008

Dear Iowa Mentoring and Induction Institute Members:

I have worked with Dennis Healy since 1982. At that time, he was a young, energetic teacher who welcomed me, the rookie, into the English Department at Dubuque Senior High School. During the intervening 26 years, I have become the principal at our school and Dennis continues to be a "young" and energetic member of our staff who welcomes rookies into the fold.

In 1982, there was no official mentoring program. Regardless, Dennis fulfilled many of functions of a mentor. He was optimistic about students; he was committed to providing a quality education in an atmosphere that was both challenging and positive; he had high standards for both his students and his colleagues.

When the mentoring program became institutionalized, Dennis was a natural to step into the role of mentor. He has the respect of other teachers, administrators, parents and students. During his years as a mentor and English department chair, he has guided a large number of young teachers. In addition, he has spent years training other mentors.

It is an honor to nominate Dennis Healy as the "Outstanding Mentor of Beginning Educator." He has been that for more than 25 years.

Sincerely,

Kim Swift

Kim Swift, Principal (and Mentee)

"My heart is singing for joy this morning. A miracle has happened! The light of understanding has shone upon my little pupil's mind, and behold, all things are changed!"   *- Anne Sullivan*

After students graduate, I rarely hear from them, which is good. I want them to look forward, not back. However, some institutions of higher learning provide opportunities for their students to reflect on their experiences and identify teachers who inspired them. The following two letters, one from a community college and one from a highly regarded liberal arts college, represent the best mail teachers can receive!

NORTHEAST IOWA COMMUNITY COLLEGE

Peosta Campus
10250 Sundown Road · Peosta, IA 52068-9703
563.556.5110 · 800.728.7367 · Fax 563.556.5058 · www.nicc.edu

student driven...community focused

May 7, 2007

Mr. Dennis Healy
Dubuque Senior High School
1800 Clarke Drive.
Dubuque, IA 52001

Dear Mr. Healy:

"Teachers affect eternity; they can never tell where their influence stops" - Henry Brooks Adams.

Undoubtedly, your influence on your students never stops because you have been recognized once again this year by one of your former students now attending Northeast Iowa Community College as an influential person in that student's life.

Each year, we at Northeast Iowa Community College offer our students the opportunity to identify those teachers who have impacted the students' lives for the better. You have received this well-deserved distinction once again. Your hard work, dedication, and sincere concern for your students is appreciated by them, sometimes more than you will ever realize.

Heather Brothers states this about you: "Mr. Healey always kept the class interesting and made me want to come to class. I learned a lot form Mr. Healy." Christina Less states this about you: "He was a great teacher and talked and opened his students up to talk about important issues we usually don't talk about at school." Peter Jecklin states this about you: "He made me want to be in class everyday. He had the best style of teaching I have ever encountered. He involved the class and made things interesting and fun."

You deserve to feel proud of the lasting impression you have made on your students and of the important role you play in the betterment of society. We at Northeast Iowa Community College join your former student in thanking you for your continuous dedication and inspiration. We take great pleasure in informing you of this recognition and wish you continued success in your important role as an educator.

Sincerely,

Penny Wills
President

Cindy O'Bryon
Provost, Peosta Campus

BH/dg

Calmar Campus · Peosta Campus

NICC Centers: Chickasaw County · Cresco · Delaware County · Dubuque · Oelwein · Town Clock

Carleton College

Johnson House
100 South College Street
Northfield, Minnesota 55057

Office of Admissions

October 16, 2006

507-646-4190
FAX 507-646-4526

Mr. Dennis Healy
Teacher of English
Dubuque Senior High School
1800 Clarke Drive
Dubuque IA 52001

Dear Mr. Healy:

For several decades now, we have asked each member of our new entering class to name the one secondary school teacher who has done the most to influence his or her development. I am delighted to be able to tell you that this year Mary Spraggins named you as this very special teacher. Clearly, this student is only one of many who benefit greatly from your efforts in the classroom.

We thought you might like to know that Mary joins one of the most able classes in Carleton history. The 504 members of the Class of 2010 were selected from an applicant pool of 4,466. One hundred of them are National Merit Scholars. As the enclosed profile suggests, these first year students were not only outstanding students, but were quite involved in school and community activities as well. They are students who are willing to take risks, and who are interested in and concerned about others.

May I express Carleton's sincere thanks for your dedicated efforts to inspire the creativity and independent thinking that we so enjoy in our students. As always, our faculty will do its best to continue the very fine work which you and your colleagues have begun.

Best wishes for continued success in your teaching.

Sincerely yours,

Paul Thiboutot
Dean of Admissions

PT:kjh
cc: Principal
Enc: Class of 2010 Profile

"The mediocre teacher tells.   The good teacher explains.   The superior teacher demonstrates.   The great teacher inspires."
- William Arthur Ward

The pictures below appeared in our school's yearbook and reflect the stages of my teaching career.

Year One 1975   **Year Sixteen 1990**   **Year Thirty-Two 2006**

This candid photo, taken by a student, captures me in a teaching moment. Note my whale coffee mug on the desk. A student gave me the mug after we read <u>One Flew Over The Cuckoo's Nest</u>.

"Our job as teachers is not to tell students what to think, it is to teach students how to think."   *- Dennis Healy*

Not all the communications I receive are complimentary. Larry Mitchell, principal at the time, put this note in my mailbox after an English Department meeting he attended at which I complained at length about a new computerized grading system our school district adopted. Unhappy with my negative attitude, he summoned me. I noted the intensity of the script, and fashioned my apology before I met with him.

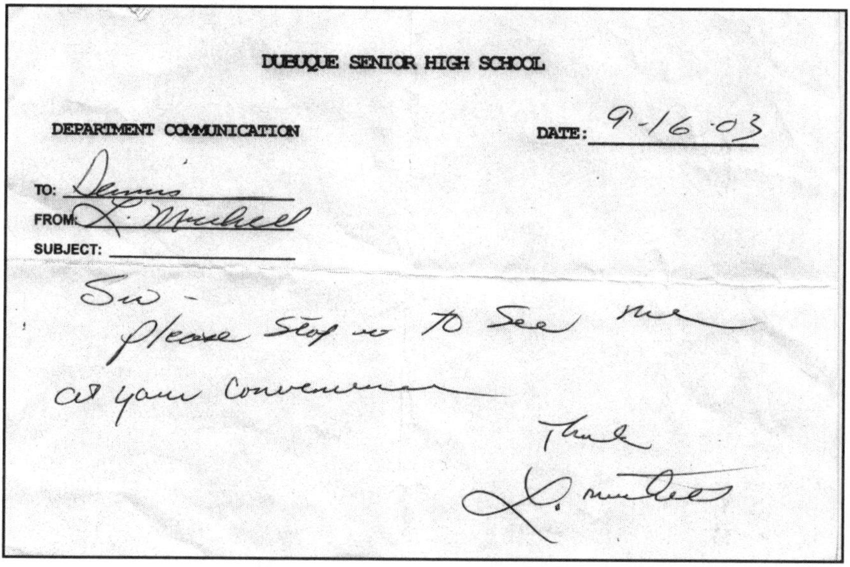

DUBUQUE SENIOR HIGH SCHOOL

DEPARTMENT COMMUNICATION   DATE: 9-16-03

TO: Dennis

FROM: L. Mitchell

SUBJECT:

Sw -
please stop in to see me
at your convenience

Thank
L. Mitchell

CASE STUDY #1

CONFISCATING NOTES FROM STUDENTS

You are teaching a large class. The students are working quietly on an assignment. Ever vigilant, you notice a student passing a note to another student.

What do you do?

Note: I handled this incident poorly.

COMMENTARY

In this case, I demanded that the student give me the note. He refused, and I sent him to the office. He muttered something unintelligible under his breath on the way out, and was sullen for several weeks after the incident.

By demanding the note, I did not address the main issue. I didn't want to read the note, I wanted the student to use class time for the assignment. By focusing on the note instead of the behavior, I escalated the incident into a personal conflict. The student probably wrote something on the note that was intended only for the recipient.

When I noticed the behavior, I should have quietly told the recipient of the note to return it to the writer, then quietly asked the writer to see me after class, at which time I would have told him to use work time for class matters.

I compounded the issue by taking it out of the class, involving an assistant principal in a relatively trivial matter.

The student and I ended the year on good terms, but it took time and effort on my part to rebuild the relationship.

In today's world text messages are more prevalent than handwritten notes. In my class guidelines, I now require that all backpacks and purses must be off the desks during class time. I believe that removing the temptation is the best policy.

CASE STUDY #2

MISTREATMENT
OF SUPPORT STAFF

You are a young teacher in your second or third year at your school. One day you are in the main office waiting to meet with the principal to schedule an observation for your evaluation. As you sit in the office, an older, experienced teacher comes into the office and begins a discussion with the receptionist, who also manages the textbooks in the building. You can hear the conversation. The teacher gives the receptionist a list of names of students who have not turned in textbooks and asks her to notify the students within the next hour. The receptionist says that she can't do that right away because she just received a shipment of supplemental texts that she needs to enter into the system and to number individually. The teacher becomes angry, raises his voice and says, "To hell with the new books. I need those textbooks now!" He then storms out of the office muttering something that includes "damn secretaries."

What would you do?

COMMENTARY

As a young teacher, there is not much you can do about this incident. Hopefully, the receptionist reports the teacher's behavior to the principal, who can then take appropriate action. Confronting an older, more experienced teacher will probably result in the teacher's telling you to mind your own business.

The best thing you can do is observe and learn. That older teacher's boorish behavior is an example of how not to treat colleagues. In Chapter 3, I discuss the significance of the support staff in a building, and how important it is to treat all personnel with respect. Teaching is a profession in which your success will be measured by the quality of the relationships you build in your career. Be part of a culture of respect, not part of a culture of disrespect.

CASE STUDY #3

DISCIPLINE
OUTSIDE THE CLASSROOM

One of the more difficult issues you will face as a young teacher is disciplining students with whom you are not acquainted outside the familiar confines of the classroom.

One afternoon at school as I walked down a nearly empty hallway, I noticed a student at his locker getting ready to leave for the day. He gathered his books and put on his hat. In our building, students are not allowed to wear hats. Ahead of me was another teacher, who spotted the student and called out, "Hey you, take off the hat!" in a stern voice.

The student turned to the teacher and said, "I'm on my way out of the building."

The teacher replied, raising his voice, "I don't care where you are going, take off the hat!"

The student pointed to the front door and said, "I'm leaving the school."

The teacher, now approaching the student, yelled, "Take off the hat, pal!"

The student, finally exasperated, yelled, "I'm leaving!"

The teacher, now in the student's face, screamed so everyone on the floor could hear, "Don't yell at me, son! We're going to the office!"

And off they went.

How would you handle a situation like this?

COMMENTARY

I saw this scene as a perfect example of how not to handle an incident like this. The teacher created three problems where one minor one existed. First, the teacher invited confrontation with his strident tone. Second, he exacerbated the situation by creating a problem unrelated to the hat policy. Two problems now exist: the hat issue (unresolved) and the discipline issue (which the student may challenge since the teacher yelled at the student for yelling at him). Third, the teacher has also involved an administrator, who will have to mediate the hostility spawned by the shouting match.

In dealing with situations like this, consider what outcome you desire, and how you will conduct yourself to achieve that end.

Instead of initiating a confrontational tone verbally, I would have approached the student, made a non-threatening statement like "How's it going?" and then walked out with the student, making small talk, and finally issuing a calm reminder of school policy regarding hats, saying something like, "Next time, remember to wait until you are outside before putting on the hat. Take it easy."

Over the years, I learned how to handle these situations without making them worse. I have two diverse sources to thank for this skill: James Fitzpatrick and American playwright August Wilson.

Fitzpatrick provided one of the most meaningful in-service sessions of my career when he talked to our staff about how to deal with discipline. Using example after example from his experiences as a dean and principal, his major theme was to avoid "pumping up" situations like the one I describe above. His advice to us when we came across a situation which needed intervention, was to ask, "What's going on?" in a non-threatening tone. This question usually stops whatever behavior is taking place, and asks for an explanation, rather than causing a confrontation.

I have used this technique many times and found it to be successful at first. But I lacked a reply when a student said, "He started it," or "She called me a bitch first." August Wilson saved me at this point. His plays, which chronicle the African-American experience in the 20th century, are replete with complex dialogue. His characters are adept at keeping conversations on topic. If a character digresses in a conversation by sidestepping a question, the questioner replies with something like this: "That's not what we're talking about. We're talking about..." So, when students replied with the above comments, I simply replied, "I didn't ask who started it. I asked what's going on," or "I didn't ask who called who a bitch, I asked what's going on." Students are usually confused at this point because I am not accusing anyone of anything. I simply want to know what they are doing, then tell them why they shouldn't do it.

As you become more experienced, you will become more adept at handling out-of-classroom situations. My advice is to focus on changing the behavior, not on how tough you are.

CASE STUDY #4

REEFER MADNESS

As you near the end of your student teaching semester, your cooperating teacher invites you and your fiancée to his home for dinner. Your cooperating teacher has been wonderful: understanding, supportive, and helpful. He has a strong rapport with his students because of his knowledge and because he's hip. You admire his ability to relate to his students.

When you and your fiancée arrive for dinner, your cooperating teacher, who prepared most of the meal, offers you a beer, which you accept, then he asks you to join him in the den while his wife puts the finishing touches on the preparation.

When you sit down, the cooperating teacher opens a drawer and takes out a pipe. He asks you if you would like to smoke some marijuana with him to, as he says, "Whet your appetite." Although you know people who smoke occasionally, you do not.

What do you do?

- **Refuse, then report the teacher to the principal?**

- **Refuse, saying that you do not indulge?**

- **Agree, only to be sociable?**

- **Leave with your fiancée immediately to avoid the uncomfortable situation?**

COMMENTARY

Strange as it may seem, this scenario could actually unfold. In fact, I know a teacher (then a student teacher) who experienced what I describe above.

The obvious choice is to politely refuse, stating that you do not smoke marijuana, then hope that dinner is ready soon to avoid the awkwardness of the moment. Too many complications arise from engaging in illegal activity. This teacher crosses the line in asking you to break the law. The controlling concept in situations like this is to avoid anything that could jeopardize your chances of employment. This philosophy includes any behavior which is illegal, including drinking excessively. Remaining sober also lessens the chances of your saying something which you later regret.

The uncontrollable variable is the cooperating teacher. He may inadvertently refer to the evening in the faculty lounge. I don't believe you want to be known as the pot-smoking student teacher. The teacher may be looking for sources for procuring marijuana, so a qualified refusal to be polite and not seem hip–"I did smoke until I started student teaching,"–may not end your dilemma.

Turning in the teacher could result in more trouble than you wish to take on before you begin interviewing for jobs. The teacher could deny the incident (there are no witnesses except for your fiancée and the cooperating teacher's wife), and create trouble for you at evaluation time, including his letter of recommendation.

The relationship between a student teacher and a cooperating teacher exists on a continuum from mentor to adversary. Conduct yourself at all times so that you can defend your actions and decisions, and have documentation whenever possible.

CASE STUDY #5

INAPPROPRIATE COMMUNICATION IN THE CLASSROOM

You start a class as usual by taking attendance and directing students to begin an assignment. As the students begin to work, a white male student looks at a female African American student across the room and says, in a sarcastic tone, "Hey, _____, what are you doin' after school, hangin' with the other hos and bitches?" The student does not respond, but is embarrassed and withdraws for the rest of the period.

What do you do?

COMMENTARY

This actually happened in a class I taught. The student who made the comment had a history of discipline problems, and the student to whom he directed the remark was a quiet, steady young woman.

This young man's behavior was abusive and harassing. In our school, it could be treated as an assault. I immediately spoke to the student, saying something like, "Mr. _____, that will be the last time we hear anything like that from you. Do you understand?" He did and was quiet for the rest of the period. At the end of the period, privately, I told him that his comments were not only unacceptable, but constituted harassment and that I intended to report him to the principal. He said, "Whatever." I also spoke to the young woman and told her what I intended to do. She said, "Thanks."

I did report the student. I filled out a harassment complaint form on the student. With the entire class as witnesses, he had no defense. He was charged with harassment. He was not a problem after that. In fact, he dropped out of school before the end of the year.

Filing for harassment is a serious act. In this case, I had clear reason to. Had the young woman asked me not to, I would have told her that I told the student that I was filing the harassment charge, and that she had no further responsibility.

As educators, we must protect our classrooms and our students from bullying and harassment. Schools must be safe. If we don't ensure that safety, we run the risk of fighting the discipline battle at the expense of instruction. We owe our students the right to learn without fear.

CASE STUDY #6

DEALING WITH SUBSTANCE ABUSE

You supervise a study hall for students who are at risk. Although the study hall is small, you must oversee students' work and academic progress daily. Early into the semester, one of your students displays signs of marijuana use: bloodshot eyes, slow reaction to questions, and the odor of marijuana on his clothes.

Almost daily, he asks to use the restroom. One day when he comes back the odor of pot is so evident that other students look at each other and smirk. After class, you talk privately to the student, asking directly if he is using marijuana. He denies it.

The next time he asks to use the restroom, you have another teacher cover your class while you check on the student. When you enter the restroom, you smell pot and see the student coming out of a stall still holding a small pipe.

What do you do?

- **Take him immediately to the assistant principal's office for discipline?**

- **Take him immediately to the school nurse and treat his case as a medical problem first?**

- **Confiscate his pipe and call the police from your room?**

- **Tell him that you will refer him to drug counseling, and if he does, you will not report the incident?**

COMMENTARY

Although the first choice is probably the most prudent, I took the student to the nurse's office. On the way, I told him that he had a problem. When he said he didn't, I told him that at some point he had become a habitual user and that, yes, he had a substance abuse problem. I told him that was why we were heading for the nurse. I wanted him to recognize that my primary concern was that he receive treatment. I also knew that the nurse would notify the assistant principal after she examined him. The nurse examined him and referred him to treatment, then notified the assistant principal for discipline. I also gave the pipe to the nurse, who gave it to the assistant principal when he came for the student.

The last two options are not wise because use of illegal substances on school grounds is a serious offense, and should always be handled through school channels, not personally. If a school official discovered that you didn't report this incident, it could be grounds for discipline.

CASE STUDY #7

PLAGIARISM

You are teaching a class which requires a research paper. Students must meet requirements along the way regarding outlining, note taking, documenting sources, writing a draft, and making corrections on the draft. One of your students lags in all these areas, but when the draft is due, he produces an excellent paper.

As you look the paper over, you notice that while the paper is on a contemporary topic, none of the references is within the last three years. Then you make a scary discovery. You go back into your files of excellent research papers, and notice that the student has copied his sister's research paper, submitted four years ago, word for word!

This is an unambiguous example of plagiarism.

What do you do?

COMMENTARY

Somewhere guidelines exist for the consequences of plagiarism. You may have them in your class guidelines. Your department may have them. Your building may have them. Your district may have them. Regardless, the student must face the consequences of a serious ethical lapse. If written guidelines exist and have been distributed in writing to the students, your task is easy: simply administer the sanctions as they exist.

But what do you do if you find the school's punishment is either more lenient or harsher than what you want to administer? Depending on how much you have shared about this incident, you should seriously consider if you plan to deviate from the accepted punishment. If you have contacted the principal, assistant principal, or guidance counselor, and you write a discipline notice, your options are limited.

Here's what I did. Since there were no specific rules governing plagiarism, and since it was my first encounter with plagiarism, I consulted with several teachers I respected before I made a decision. Then I talked to the student, showed him his sister's paper and his to make my case, and he admitted to cheating. I told him that he had a zero for the paper, but he could write another and receive partial credit. The critical point here is that I wanted him to do the assignment. Simply assigning a zero dealt with the offense, but the student did not do the work necessary to demonstrate that he could research a topic and write about it. He did the assignment and got a D. He passed the class, but his A- before the research paper dropped to a C+ at the end of the course. He learned his lesson and he learned how to properly research.

Years later, I saw him at a restaurant. He was a successful business man. Before my wife and I ordered, the server brought over a very nice bottle of wine to our table. "I didn't order this?" I said. The server replied, "The gentleman over there ordered it. He said to tell you that you'd know why. He said he owed you."

CASE STUDY #8

STRESS CARRIERS IN THE FACULTY LOUNGE

You are a young teacher, in your third or fourth year. Your career is going well, and students respect you as a skilled and caring teacher. The toughest part of your day, however, is your duty-free lunch period in the faculty lounge. Two teachers dominate the discussions in the lounge, and they are both consistently negative. Their discussions center on a few favorite themes: how ill-prepared students are; how lazy they are; how their parents don't care; how they won't do homework; how little they learned in previous grades; how poorly behaved they are.

You do not enjoy lunch. In fact, you have to refocus before returning to class, where you find little evidence of the traits the teachers harp on in the lounge.

What do you do?

- **Stop going to the lounge for lunch?**

- **Confront the teachers on their negative attitudes?**

COMMENTARY

I despise disparaging comments about students in the faculty lounge. One day as a teacher bemoaned the deficiencies of his students, some of whom I had and who were doing fine, I interrupted him. "For a change, how about telling us about something good that a student did today?" He looked at me, dumbfounded. Since he didn't speak, I continued, "We're all here to help students succeed. What do you hope to accomplish by running down students so often? I, for one, am tired of hearing it." He was silent, and did not ramble about students as long as I was there.

I was able to get away with a confrontational tone because I know the teacher and he knows that I have credibility in the building (I taught his daughter). Once you achieve some standing in your school for being an effective teacher, there may be times when you must take a stand against negativity. There were young teachers at the table that day. I wanted them to know that it's hard to be a good teacher when your free time consists of saying disparaging things about students.

If you are a young teacher, do not take the bait. No matter how challenging things are, do not become a force of negativity. It may feel cathartic to unburden your frustrations about students in the faculty lounge, but for the sake of the building, you are better off venting with your mentor or another colleague than poisoning the collective atmosphere of the lounge.

CASE STUDY #9

BREAKING UP FIGHTS

You have just finished lunch in the teacher section of the cafeteria. You have some work to do to prepare for your next class, so you leave a little early. You take your tray to the appropriate area, and as you exit the cafeteria, a fight breaks out between two girls immediately in front of you. The girls are already engaged; one has punched the other and they are now locked in battle.

What do you do?

- **Find an administrator?**

- **Break up the fight yourself?**

- **Tell students to break up the fight while you find an administrator?**

COMMENTARY

Whether you have playground supervision, lunchroom supervision, hall duty, or if you are in the halls, you will eventually encounter a fight. If you don't, you work in a privileged learning environment. I have learned several key things about breaking up fights:

1) Determine how advanced the fight is before charging in to break it up. Twice in my career, I have seen teachers try to come between combatants, only to be punched as they did. In some cases, calling the principal from the nearest phone is the best policy.

2) Fights usually begin with insults, and then move to threats, and then move to the physical stage. One of my techniques is to raise my voice louder than the would-be pugilists. It diverts them (and the students who want to see the fight). I also use very direct and dramatic diction as a distraction. I won't divulge what I say, but in nearly all cases it shifts attention from the fighters to me.

3) If you get into the center of a fight, think only of survival. The incident I describe above actually took place several years ago. As I was leaving the lunchroom two young women went at each other only a few feet from me. Instinctively, I got between them, then learned I was in danger. One girl had the other by the hair, and the other had her enemy by the throat. I needn't mention the names they called each other. As the three of us struggled, we fell to the floor. A large group of students gathered around us, cheering our efforts. I called for help, but this lunchroom melee was far too entertaining. Finally, two administrators arrived, separated the girls and saved me. As I rose from the floor, the students cheered my efforts. I wished they had shown such support when I was writhing on the floor.

4) Finally, talk to your principal about appropriate methods of intervention, and talk to colleagues about what they do in the event of a fight. In most cases you will not have time ponder your move. Be ready when the time comes!

CASE STUDY #10

CREATING AND MAINTAINING REASONABLE CLASS GUIDELINES

At the beginning of the year, a teacher hands out his class guidelines and policies. In one section, he clearly states that students bring paper and pen and pencil to class daily, and that failure to bring these items will result in zeros on tests or quizzes.

Two weeks into the marking period, the teacher gives a chapter test. One student forgets his pencil and pen. The teacher says, "Sorry, you'll have to take a zero on the test. Maybe this will help you remember the next time."

What is your reaction to this scenario?

- **Good for the teacher! We must teach students to be responsible.**

- **The teacher is justified in giving the student a zero because the clearly identified the pen and pencil rule in the class guidelines.**

- **The teacher's guidelines are unnecessarily harsh because they punish the student by denying him a chance to demonstrate his knowledge.**

COMMENTARY

This incident actually occurred at my school. It brings up the critical question: What do you as a teacher want to achieve by having a rule like that? In my estimation, the teacher's desire for power interfered with the student's right to learn. Having a rule like that creates a Catch-22 situation: If the teacher gives the student a pen or pencil, he compromises his policies; if he stands firm and gives the student a zero, the student has no chance to show what he learned.

In my view, such a rule creates unnecessary conflict. In my class, I have a number of pencils and pens, and if students forget theirs, I loan them to the students, but only if the students provide collateral. I'll accept almost anything: student IDs, cell phones, billfolds, purses, car keys. I never lose pens or pencils and the students complete the assignments.

This case study shows the importance of constructing class guidelines that avoid potentially negative situations. How do you think that student felt sitting in the classroom while his classmates took the test? How do you think he felt about his teacher? We do not need to create shameful scenes in our classrooms. As I've said before, we need to find ways for students to succeed.

CASE STUDY #11

THE INTERVIEW TRAP

You arrive at a school to interview for a job that you feel is an ideal teaching opportunity. The interview goes well at the outset; your preparation allows you to answer quickly and concisely.

After a half hour, the principal abruptly asks, "Are you married?" Taken aback, you ponder the question. Before you can answer, the principal says, "Imagine you are the principal. Two of my married faculty members are having an affair, and the whole school knows about it. What would you do if you were the principal? In other words, what do you think of faculty members committing adultery?"

How would you respond?

COMMENTARY

This uncomfortable situation poses many challenges. Since you want the job badly, you want to answer in a way that satisfies the principal. You may overlook the impropriety of the questions. You may feel that if you refuse to answer the questions because they are inappropriate, the principal will see you as a potential troublemaker and write you off.

By reviewing a standard list of questions you might encounter in an interview, you may overlook how to respond to questions that are neither pertinent nor fair.

In my estimation, the best responses to these questions is to answer the first with a flat "Yes," or "No," and do not elaborate. On the second question, say that you are unfamiliar with the situation, and add that you do not judge people you don't know. If the principal dislikes your responses and does not offer you the job, consider yourself lucky. The teaching position may have been desirable, but the principal's line of questioning suggests that the working conditions could be undesirable. A principal who scrutinizes her or his teachers' private lives and comments on them to complete strangers may not provide the environment conducive to your early growth as a teacher. You will be better off with a less appealing teaching assignment and a caring, supportive principal who creates a positive and collegial culture in her or his building.

CASE STUDY #12

SUPERVISION

You supervise one of your school's computer labs. It is an active area. Teachers bring classes in to work on essays, do internet research, and create power point presentations. You also supervise individual students who come to the computer lab to work on assignments for other teachers.

Your supervision is the last period of the day. One Friday, a science class works on an internet assignment on endangered species, using twenty-five of the thirty computers. Two "walk-ins," students with passes from their teachers to make up late work, are also busy.

At the end of the period, all students leave except one. As you check to see that all computers are logged off, the student continues to work. You tactfully tell him that the period is over and that you must close the computer lab. He asks you to let him to stay to finish his assignment, which is already late. He says he's almost finished, and adds that he has no computer at home and will not be able to finish the assignment unless he stays.

What do you do?

- **Stay with him until he finishes, even though you have other commitments?**

- **Tell him that his teacher must supervise him because the school has no after-school program, and that you will call the teacher's room and ask her to come to the lab?**

- **Tell him he must leave, because you cannot allow students to be in the computer lab unsupervised?**

- **Tell him that he can stay, but he must turn off the lights and close the door tightly when he leaves?**

COMMENTARY

The first three are all acceptable options; the last one is not. This situation actually happened at our school. The teacher allowed the student to stay in the lab unsupervised, and a half hour later, technology representatives from the school district called our administrators and informed them that someone was downloading pornography in that computer lab. One of our assistant principals went immediately to the lab and caught the violator.

The primary lesson in this incident is a crucial one in teaching: DO NOT LEAVE STUDENTS UNSUPERVISED AT ANY TIME, ESPECIALLY WHEN THEY ARE UNDER YOUR SUPERVISION.

You are under no obligation to supervise the student beyond your contract stipulations, unless you voluntarily agree to do so. In the first option, for example, you are well within your rights to tell the student to leave. You may have to pick up your children, you may have one of your students coming to your room for help, you may be supervising an activity after school, and you may simply need to leave because you are tired. If you must leave and the student implores you to let him stay, call the student's teacher. If the teacher cannot supervise, you must close the computer lab.

CASE STUDY #13

PROBLEM SOLVING WITH THE PRINCIPAL

Parent teacher conferences are a stressful time for teachers. On all levels—elementary, middle school, and high school—teachers can work for hours without a break seeing parent after parent or guardian after guardian. While most conferences go well, the teacher never knows how parents will react to their children's performances and the teacher's interpretation of those performances. One year at our high school during fall conferences, our principal decided to take the conference days off and go hunting with some friends in another part of the state.

When conferences started, teachers quickly learned that their principal was not there. After conferences ended, teachers complained about the principal's absence. The principal caught wind of these complaints and was quite upset.

He called me into his office to tell me that he was calling a faculty meeting to say that he had every right to take the days off and that he was tired of hearing about these whiners and complainers. He said people who were upset should tell him personally about it. I could tell he was angry and that the faculty meeting would be a dressing down session.

I believe I handled this session well.

What did I say to the principal?

COMMENTARY

I knew some of the faculty members who complained. In fact, I was disappointed that our principal was not there while we were meeting with the parents, and I had shared this with several colleagues.

For the principal, conferences are important in several ways: they provide an opportunity for public relations; they provide an opportunity for parents with concerns to talk to the person in charge; they provide an opportunity for the principal to support teachers who may be unnecessarily confronted by irate parents; and they provide an opportunity for the principal to interact with both parents and teachers in the fluid atmosphere of conferences.

When our principal told me his plans to give the faculty a piece of his mind, I thought it would create a negative reaction from the staff. Why should those who didn't complain be subjected to his wrath? Why criticize those who wanted his leadership at conferences?

I asked him, "What do you want to get out of this meeting? People in this building see you as their leader. I think they were disappointed that they didn't have their leader for two pretty challenging nights." He thought for a minute, and said, "Thanks, I'll think about this."

He cancelled the meeting. The next day, I got a note from him thanking me for giving him my perspective, and for helping him make "the right decision" about canceling the meeting. I was glad that he sought my opinion and I was glad that he listened to me!

CASE STUDY #14

COMING TO THE AID OF A COLLEAGUE

A colleague of yours is in his early years in the classroom. He is also an activity sponsor. He takes a group of students to a state competition out of town. While he and the team are there, his fiancée stays with him at the hotel where he and the team are staying. In fact, she stays in the same room with him.

After the group performs and returns, the principal receives an anonymous telephone call informing him of the hotel situation. Two days later, the principal calls the teacher into his office and without warning, tells him that the school district plans to fire him.

You are also a young activities sponsor. The teacher comes to you and asks what he should do. You refer him to the representative of the local teachers' association.

In the meantime, other activities sponsors find out about the nature of the phone call and the abruptness of the meeting with the principal. People feel that the young teacher was not treated fairly.

What would you do in this situation?

- **Organize the other activities sponsors and register a protest to the superintendent?**

- **Let the teachers' association deal with it?**

- **Notify an attorney friend for advice?**

- **Side with the principal to show support of strong ethics?**

COMMENTARY

This incident actually took place early in my career. The teacher was a coach, and he was so naïve, he didn't believe that having his fiancée stay in the same room was a violation of ethics. Clearly, he was myopic. However, the circumstances surrounding his situation—an anonymous call, and an "ambush" in the principal's office—made all of the coaches feel that they could be fired as the result of any unsubstantiated report.

The coaches met as a group, and in an unusual display of unity, twenty-five of the twenty-six coaches resigned from their coaching positions. I consulted with two attorney friends who advised me in the matter. I became the spokesperson for the coaches, and we made our case. To my surprise, I appeared on several television stations, explaining the coaches' stance. I was also interviewed by the local television station and newspaper the night the school board rendered its decision.

The coach was not fired. He was suspended for a month without pay. Since then, he has distinguished himself as an outstanding coach and has had a successful career in the classroom as well.

As I look back on the experience, I realize that all of us were standing up for ourselves as well as our colleague. It was a rare moment of unity and rebellion, one I'll never forget. Shortly after the issue was resolved, the principal visited me in my room. He asked me if the coaches would forgive him. I told him, "Time will tell." He never did regain the full confidence of the coaches.

CASE STUDY #15

THE JOURNAL NIGHTMARE

Journaling is a popular writing activity not only in the language arts, but also in other curricular areas as a means to enhance literacy and writing across the curriculum. There is a wide range of responses among journal writers, from the unresponsive to the indifferent to the competent to the highly verbal and analytical. Any of these groups can include students who are self-disclosing, sometimes to an alarming degree.

Imagine that early in your career you have a journaling requirement in your class. One student writes extensive and serious entries about the personal issues of her life—dating, her parents, her classes, her job, her weekends. One Thursday night as you settle in to read journals, you select hers. After a page of processing the week, she divulges that her parents are manufacturing, selling, and using methamphetamine and that life at home has become unbearable.

What is the first thing you do when you arrive at school the next morning?

- **Call the police?**

- **Take the journal to the guidance counselor?**

- **Call the girl's parents immediately?**

- **Find the girl in school and ask to speak to her?**

- **Report the incident to the school nurse and the assistant principal?**

COMMENTARY

The greatest problem with journaling is the possibility of a student's disclosing information for which you, as teacher, are a mandatory reporter. It is essential to know your state's definition of child abuse, its categories (see below), and its laws governing juveniles. As teacher, you must clearly state to your classes (in writing) that while journal entries are confidential, you must suspend that confidentiality in cases for which you are a mandatory reporter. Laying that groundwork at the beginning of the term will make students aware of the exceptions to confidentiality.

For example, in the state of Iowa, teachers are mandatory reporters and are required to report this incident to the Department of Human Services, since it is included in the state's definition of child abuse. It may be advisable to consult with other members of the school team, such as the guidance counselor or school nurse, who may know more about the family situation and then determine who among you will make the report. While the possibility exists that the girl in this case may not be telling the truth, it is generally better to err on the side of reporting. If something were to happen to the girl, you may be liable if you have knowledge of possible abuse and do not make a report. It is best practice to make the principal or assistant principal aware of the situation and that a report is being filed. In some cases of reporting suspected abuse, you may choose to talk to the student and/or parent and notify them that you are making a report; however, this is not required by law and may complicate cases involving illegal drugs in the home.

The 9 categories of child abuse in Iowa are listed below. These categories vary from state to state. As a teacher you may be required to attend training regarding the law in your state.

The 9 Categories of Child Abuse in Iowa

- Physical Abuse
- Mental Injury
- Sexual Abuse
- Denial of Critical Care
- Child Prostitution
- Presence of Illegal Drugs
- Manufacturing or Possession of Illegal Substances
- Bestiality in the Presence of a Minor
- Cohabiting with a registered sex offender

CASE STUDY #16

EXCESSIVE VISITS TO GUIDANCE

You have a large class, and managing attendance is challenging. Midway into the first marking period, you notice that a certain student comes to class late at least once a week with a pass from his guidance counselor. You also discover that on past several occasions when the student was absent, he spent the entire period with his counselor. You notice no demonstrable emotional problems with the student, and he completes his work, but has fallen behind because of the time he spends with his counselor.

What do you do?

- **Complain to the principal?**

- **Talk to the student to find out why he misses so much class?**

- **Talk to the guidance counselor to find out if the student has some problem of which you are unaware?**

- **Confront the guidance counselor and demand that the student not miss any more class time?**

- **Call the student's parents to report the tardies and absences and to inform them that the student's grade has fallen because of the visits to the counselor?**

COMMENTARY

This problem centers on communication. For you, the issue is that the student's visits to the counselor are affecting his grade, and the counselor has not communicated the reasons for the visits. The first thing to explore is the cause of the tardies and absences. Does the student dislike your class and want to get out of it? Is there another student in the class who threatens the student? Is the counselor unaware that the student is missing class? Does the student have a serious personal problem and confides only with the counselor? Has the counselor promised to keep the nature of the sessions confidential?

To keep the lines of communication as direct as possible, talk to the student first, asking him what's going on. You might say, "I'm concerned about your grade and your attendance. You've come late three times in the last three weeks with passes from your counselor, and you've been absent from class twice because you were with your counselor. What's going on? Is there something I should know? If you are not prepared to learn, I want to know so we can do something about it." This approach does not threaten the student; rather, it is as an expression of concern for the student's success. If the student is forthcoming about the reasons for the visits, and if the visits involve an issue which can include you in its resolution, you have done well.

You must also talk to the counselor to see why he/she must see your student during class time, and to explain that the visits have negatively affected the student's grade. Maintaining a problem solving tone is also crucial in this conversation. Showing concern for the student's success and asking to be part of the solution are critical to resolving the problem. Using questions like, "How can we resolve this?" or "What can we do to best meet the student's emotional and academic needs?" will keep the discussion focused on the student. Remember that your objectives are to raise both the student's and the counselor's levels of concern, to make them aware of your perspective, and to show your desire for the ultimate success of the student.

You must also consider preventative measures to avoid such situations. In my class guidelines, I include the following statement about guidance services: **Class time is not to be used for visits to the guidance office. If you have an emergency, come to class and I will make the necessary arrangements for you. If you visit guidance during class without seeing me first, I will consider it an unexcused absence unless the counselor confirms that the visit was an emergency.**

CASE STUDY #17

THE INATTENTIVE STUDENT

You are a middle school math teacher. As you present a lesson on a new concept, you notice a student sitting near the back reading a book. This student is highly proficient in math, and when you ask the student to put away the book and pay attention, he says he already knows the concept.

What do you do at that point?

- Say immediately, "It doesn't matter, put your book away?"

- Allow the student to continue to read, then talk to him individually after class?

- Send the impudent student to the principal' office?

- Throw an eraser at him to get his attention?

- None of the above?

COMMENTARY

This is a difficult situation. From the student's point of view, he doesn't need instruction on a concept he already understands. From the teacher's standpoint, a student's lack of attention can lead others to tune out and create an even larger problem.

In my estimation, resolving this issue involves communication, assessment, and evaluation.

First, I would calmly stop the lesson and ask the student to speak to me in the hall.

Second, away from the students, I would ask the student why he was reading a book. When he says that he already knows the concept, I would commend him for that, then offer to explore alternatives for him, such as enrichment, placement in a more challenging math group, or individualizing instruction for him.

Third, I would ask him to pay attention for the rest of the period, after which we would explore accelerating his math learning.

Taking this conversation out of the classroom (keeping one eye on the rest of the students!) reduces the tension of a confrontation which other students do not need to witness. You also show understanding of the student's behavior, and you are constructive rather confrontational. If the student is reasonable, he will comply with your request for attention for the rest of the period.

CASE STUDY #18

SENSITIVE PERSONAL ISSUES

During my years as a cross country coach, I encountered a number of sensitive personal issues with the young women I coached. One Saturday morning, one of my runners, a sophomore, came to practice with a black eye. She was also upset and appeared to have been crying.

Before we started practice, I called her aside and asked her if everything was OK. She started to cry and said, "No, everything is not OK."

I asked her if she wanted to talk about it, and she told me, "My brother beat me up last night."

This young woman was a talented young runner, but she came from a challenging background. She was in a single parent home, and her brother had a history of fighting and was involved with racist peers.

I knew what action I needed to take, and I believe I did the right thing. What did I do?

- **Call the young woman's mother and ask to talk to her?**

- **Call the residence and ask to talk to the young woman's brother to see if the story was credible?**

- **Tell the young woman to tell me if her brother hit her again?**

- **Report the incident to the school nurse?**

COMMENTARY

Since the incident occurred between siblings, and did not involve a caretaker, it was not a case of child abuse. In this case, I am considered a permissive reporter. I am not bound by law to report the incident, but I did report the incident to our school nurse because the girl was bruised and emotionally distraught. After investigation by the department of social services, the young woman was removed from the home, and finished the remainder of her high school years in a foster home. She graduated on time, and remained on the cross country team.

If the girl told me that her father had struck her, I would have been a mandatory reporter. Her wounds were visible, which constituted sufficient evidence to report the incident.

In Iowa, child abuse occurs when a primary caretaker abuses a child under 18 years old. There are nine categories of child abuse in Iowa. (see page 215)

Know your state's child abuse code, and know your school district's policies regarding mandatory reporting and permissive reporting– you may save a life.

CASE STUDY #19

DEALING WITH A PARENT DURING THE SCHOOL DAY

In mid-September one year, I was teaching my fifth period class when our activities coordinator appeared at my door with a woman. I stopped class and went to the door. The activities coordinator introduced the woman as the mother of one of my freshmen cross country runners, then walked away. I thought she came to explain that her daughter couldn't run in the meet that day because the girl was sick or some family issue had come up.

Instead, the woman expressed concern that it was too hot that day, and her daughter might dehydrate and collapse at the race site. She wondered if I knew enough about competing and hydration.

I was dumbfounded. The high that day was barely 80 degrees, and the team had practiced in similar conditions for the past month. I explained to the woman that I had over twenty years experience in coaching cross country and was a competitive runner myself. I assured her that I would take all necessary precautions to ensure that the runners were hydrated and that I would look for signs of dehydration during the races. She finally left, still expressing some concern about the conditions that day.

After nearly five minutes, I returned to my class.

What would you do as a follow up to such a situation?

- **Thank the administrator for directing the parent to your classroom?**

- **Tell the administrator to notify you before sending parents to your room during the school day?**

- **Go to the principal and complain about the administrator's actions?**

COMMENTARY

When my class broke for lunch, I went immediately to the activities coordinator and told him not to send parents to my room during the school day unless it was an emergency that he could not handle. He could have talked to the parent in his office, and assured her that I was experienced in running in all types of weather and that her daughter was safe to compete.

The girl ran well that day. My students and I did not need to lose five minutes of class time. That was clearly a job that an activities coordinator should have handled himself. He did not send any more parents to my classroom after that.

CASE STUDY #20

A STRUGGLING STUDENT TEACHER

You have been teaching just long enough to qualify for supervision of a student teacher. As the year begins, you and the student teacher establish a working relationship. She observes intently and asks pertinent questions about classroom management, instruction, and planning. As the date draws close for her to take over her first classes, she becomes noticeably nervous. You work with her on lesson plans every day, and cover, day by day, the first week. Two days before she takes over, you ask to see the lesson plans. She has none. She says it's really hard to think of how to fill the class period. You ask, "Are you ready to teach the class?" She responds, "I don't think so."

What do you do?

- **Make her teach? It's time to sink or swim!**

- **Contact her supervisor and ask for a conference with the three of you?**

- **Tell her it's OK and that she can start with the next unit?**

- **Agree to introduce the unit, then let her take over?**

COMMENTARY

This actually happened to me early in my career. Thinking that having a student teacher would reduce my teaching load and give me time to read essays during school time, I agreed to supervise one. Neither occurred. It was a rough semester. With much coaching, she took over after I introduced the unit, but struggled for the entire semester. She had serious problems with classroom management (she was too meek and passive), she had trouble with delivering lessons (she couldn't follow her lesson plans), and she had trouble with assessment (she did not return assignments in a timely fashion). She did not take over a full class load (I kept my most challenging class), and by the end, both of us were ready to part ways. I gave her an underwhelming recommendation. She did get a job the next year, but soon left the profession.

An additional problem with this situation was the response of the supervising professor at the college. She felt that for some reason, I was responsible for the student teacher's poor performance. I shared my frustrations with experienced colleagues, and they all said that I had been more than understanding of the student teacher. I was so frustrated after that experience that I did not take another student teacher for fifteen years.

CASE STUDY #21

DIRECTING STUDENTS TO MORE CHALLENGING CLASSES

You supervise a computer lab which is open to all classes. One day a special education class comes in to work on an assignment on the computers. You soon notice that one student works very efficiently and accurately. She completes her assignment without asking for assistance, then helps other students who have trouble with either the computers or their assignments.

You wonder, does this student belong in this class?

I believe I handled this situation well.

What would you do?

COMMENTARY

It's risky to assess a student on one observation. The young woman mentioned above may have been much more challenging in the classroom environment than in a computer lab.

Here's what I did.

Since she worked independently and completed her task so quickly, I determined that her placement must have been based on behavior. Yet she helped her classmates without complaint. I asked the teacher if he had considered recommending her for a transfer to a regular classroom. He said he really hadn't, and that he appreciated her assistance with the students who struggled. I asked him if he had spoken to her about transferring, and he said he hadn't.

I next spoke with the special education department chair to see if there were any reasons not to transfer the student. I told the department chair that I thought her skills and behavior supported such a change. We reviewed the student's transcript and agreed that she could be successful in a regular classroom.

Once I had the department chair's approval, I talked to the student. I found her during her free period and told her that I was impressed with her skills. She said that the assignment was easy. I asked her if she would consider transferring to a regular class, and she said she would. I asked her if she wouldn't mind my recommending that to the department chair in special education, and she said to go ahead.

The student transferred at the end of the semester and had a successful second semester in her new class. Her former teacher thanked me for making the recommendation.

A primary role for all teachers is to help students succeed, and one way to ensure students' success is to challenge them as much as we can. We must be talent scouts, looking for ways for students to maximize their skills. In our school, we believe that creating a culture of opportunity will translate into a culture of success. We must be attuned to students' talents, needs, and potential. One teacher, one class, can transform a disinterested student into an engaged, high-achieving student. This applies to the entire spectrum of students in our schools.

CASE STUDY #22

FUNDRAISERS AND REWARDS

You are a young teacher in a middle school that prides itself on providing students with field trip opportunities. In recent years, however, the school district has cut funding for such trips and placed responsibility on individual schools.

Your class is participating in a fundraiser that will subsidize a student trip to a major event in a big city. You distribute the information to your students and talk to them about the importance of raising money for the valuable educational experience.

The end of the fundraiser coincides with a major test. To reward the students who raised money, you announce that students who sold items for the fundraiser will be allowed to use their books for the test, and those who chose not to participate will not.

A student who did not raise any money objects, claiming that your decision is unfair, and says she will tell her parents.

What would you do?

- **Ignore the complaint and allow only the sellers to use their books on the test?**

- **Change the test so that sellers will have only a small advantage on it?**

- **Change your mind and allow all students to use their books?**

- **Take back the announcement and don't allow any students to use their books during the test?**

COMMENTARY

While it is good to motivate students to contribute to school fundraisers, it is discriminatory to provide participants with unfair advantages on quizzes, essays, or tests. Some students abhor fundraising, especially door-to-door solicitations, and should not be punished for that. Some students' parents will not allow their children to fundraise, and some students who are very active outside of school do not have time to comb their neighborhoods for willing buyers. Some citizens resent such solicitations, and develop negative attitudes toward schools, which are already recipients of taxpayer money. Finally, some parents buy the materials themselves to avoid having their children sell merchandise.

Whatever rewards you offer for such activities should be unrelated to evaluation.

CASE STUDY #23

STUDENT
VS.
STUDENT ASSISTANCE

You are teaching an elective course for upper classmen. One of your students has had some problems during the semester and has missed a great deal of class. On this day near the end of the semester, the student is present and is ready to take a major test. The test is crucial; the student is near failing, and needs a good performance on this test to have a chance to pass.

Ten minutes into the test, someone delivers a pass for the student from the guidance office telling the student to come immediately to the guidance area to see a counselor from a community mental health facility.

What do you do?

COMMENTARY

In this case, I had the student remain in class and finish the test. Ten minutes after the first pass arrived (I wrote "Taking test" on the first pass and sent it back with the messenger), a second one appeared with "Send IMMEDIATELY!" I ignored this one, too. After the student finished the exam, she went to the guidance office and saw the counselor.

One of our assistant principals, obviously not happy with me, spoke to me after the incident. He said that we should honor passes for such personnel. I apologized, but said that the student's grade was at stake.

To this day, I believe I did the right thing. I had the student in the classroom. I wasn't sure she'd be there the next day or the day after, for that matter. To me, her passing the class was more important than missing twenty minutes of a counseling session. I could live with the counselor's and the assistant principal's being upset with me.

The student, by the way, passed the test, passed the final and got a C in the class.

CASE STUDY #24

WORKING WITH A STUDENT TEACHER

You are an experienced teacher. You agree to supervise a student teacher for a semester. The student teacher is bright and competent, and knows the students well after only a short time. Everything is going well. The student teacher takes over several classes and creates effective lesson plans.

One day after he finishes a lesson, you remind students of some up-coming events (marking periods, parent conferences). As you talk, you notice the students smirking, smiling, and laughing. Since the material you are discussing is mundane, you quickly turn around and notice that the student teacher is mimicking you behind your back. You finish the comments, the bell rings, and the students leave.

What action do you take?

- **Teacher A thought it over, did not see it as a major issue, and let the event pass.**

- **Teacher B thought it over, formulated a response, and at the end of the day told the student teacher that what he did was inexcusable and rude. Teacher B also told the student teacher that he was considering contacting the student teacher's supervisor and requesting either a conference or a change in cooperating teachers.**

COMMENTARY

This incident actually happened to me as a cooperating teacher. I could not overlook such disrespectful and unprofessional behavior. This young man needed to realize that as a teacher he was in a professional situation. I did not report this to his supervisor, but I did tell him that I was seriously considering requesting reassignment for him. The night after our discussion (actually, it was not a discussion), he came to my house, personally apologized, and vowed to comport himself professionally for the remainder of the semester, which he did.

As professionals, teachers must insist on respectful and professional behavior from student observers and student teachers. Failure to address such behavior could result in these young people becoming undesirable colleagues. They must understand the importance of respecting colleagues, especially in front of students.

CASE STUDY #25

CREATIVE DISCIPLINE

In around my tenth year of teaching, I felt confident in the classroom. I'd moved beyond overreacting to incidents, and I had a good rapport with my students. During the fall of the year, I was writing on the board when suddenly something hit me squarely in the back of the head. Someone in the class had thrown a hacky sack and pegged me perfectly. The students were shocked and they awaited my response. I picked up the hacky and said, "Whose hacky is this?" To my surprise, a student raised his hand and acknowledged that it was his. "Thank you, Mr. _____, I'll keep this as evidence," I said, and returned immediately to the lesson.

How do you think I responded to this incident?

COMMENTARY

After the class, I crafted my plan. I conferred with one of our assistant principals. I explained the incident, and asked him if he would go along with my plan. I outlined the plan, and he agreed.

Here's what happened. The assistant principal called the student into his office, showed him the hacky, and asked if it was his. The student admitted to being the owner. Then the assistant principal told him that I had gone home from school with a severe headache and that I had also made an appointment with a physician to see if I had a concussion. The AP then told the student that the school would probably charge him with assault, and that the police would be informed. Then the AP got stern, asking the student why he would do such a dangerous thing in the classroom, especially to a teacher with whom he had a good relationship. The student was incredulous, apologetic, and very worried. "Well, I guess the next step is to call your parents," said the AP. "Oh, no, they'll kill me," said the student. His parents were upstanding people and would not tolerate any nonsense.

At that moment, I knocked on the AP's door and entered. "What?" asked the student. I explained to him that I thought his little prank deserved a response in kind. "So all that stuff about the concussion and assault charges isn't true?" he asked. "No," said the AP, "but I think you have some serious apologizing to do, the sooner the better."

The student apologized, then asked what punishment he would receive. I said, "None this time, but if anything like that happens again, I will show no mercy." "Understood," said the student. We had no further problems, and he finished the semester with a very good grade.

The assistant principal saw me later on the day of the incident. He said, "That was the best intervention I've ever been associated with!" and we both laughed.

Twenty years after the incident, I received an e-mail from the student. It is reprinted in Chapter 7.

CASE STUDY #26

WHEN A MENTOR FAILS

You are a seasoned veteran. As a natural progression to your career, you become involved in your district's mentoring program for new teachers. You receive training to mentor new teachers, you receive further training to train teachers to mentor new teachers, and you are your building's leader in mentoring issues. Each year you mentor a new teacher, train twenty to forty teachers to become mentors, and you work with the principal to place mentors with new teachers in your building.

Near the end of the first semester, a new teacher approaches you with some disturbing news. His mentor has failed to establish contact with him and they do not meet on a regular basis. Even after he asked the mentor to meet to discuss some challenges he was facing, the mentor did not follow through, canceling several meetings and not showing up for an after-school meeting.

With a semester of neglect (mentoring is a paid position) against him, it is obvious that the mentor is not performing satisfactorily.

What do you do?

COMMENTARY

Many school districts have someone in charge of mentoring. It could be a district administrator, or it could be a regional administrator. In any case, mentor neglect cannot go unreported. New teachers deserve a caring and reliable mentor. As a building leader, it is your responsibility to contact the person in charge of mentoring and inform that person of the situation. In the case I outlined above, the new teacher was reluctant to notify the mentoring coordinator because he feared that the coordinator would then discipline the mentor and the relationship would be jeopardized. The new teacher came to me with the problem. I contacted the coordinator, who worked with the new teacher to resolve some of the issues he faced. In fact, the coordinator assumed the mentoring role for the second semester. I also provided support when needed. The assigned mentor provided minimal support for the rest of the year.

Sadly, the new teacher was accosted by an irrational parent at spring conferences, but didn't feel confident confiding in his mentor. I did what I could at the time of the incident, but I knew that the mentor had abdicated his responsibility. I conveyed this to the coordinator, and he assured me that the mentor would never mentor again.

The new teacher survived, but his year should have been less traumatic. He could have easily quit at the end of the year. If you make a commitment to assist new teachers, follow through. It is shameful to neglect those who need our knowledge, wisdom, and compassion.

CASE STUDY #27

HELPING A NEW TEACHER

You are an experienced, well-respected teacher. One day while you re-search an upcoming unit in the main learning center, a group of twenty students noisily comes in and sits down at six tables near you. They continue to talk when they sit down, and the learning center supervisor has to ask them to be quiet.

After two more minutes, the teacher, in his second year, arrives and gives the students general instructions about the research assignment. The students, already engaged in conversation, pay little attention, and are slow to begin the task. One student has a question, and the teacher goes to the student's table to help, turning his back on the rest of the class. The chatter continues. At the table nearest you, four young women make small talk. One checks her makeup. Another checks for messages on her cell phone. Since you can't get any work done, you glance at the other tables and notice little engagement.

The learning center supervisor approaches the area, obviously upset.

You leave, unable to get any work done.

What do you do in this situation?

- **Let the teacher and the learning center supervisor work it out?**

- **Intervene and tell the students to quiet down and get to work?**

- **Talk to the teacher about the matter?**

- **Tell the principal about the incident?**

- **If you were to talk to the teacher, what would you tell him/her?**

COMMENTARY

I observed a similar situation. As I left the learning center, I knew I had to talk to the teacher. Fortunately, he came to me at the end of the day. He was upset because the learning center supervisor told him that if his students did not behave better the next time they came as a class, he would not be able to bring classes to the learning center any more. He thought he was treated unfairly.

I asked him how productive the class was during the period. He said he didn't know. I then asked him about the table with the four young women friends. He grimaced. Then I asked him if he checked for progress at the end of the period. He grimaced again.

He finally asked, "What should I do the next time to avoid being banished?"

I told him he needed to do four things:
1) Assign seats at the tables before going to the learning center.
2) Arrive at the learning center with the students, not two or three minutes later.
3) Monitor the class at all times, keeping an eye on everyone and checking for engagement during the period.
4) Check students' progress at the end of the period.

The following day he came to my room at the end of the day and thanked me several times for my suggestions. He said the day went much better in the learning center. "I will do all of those things from now on!" he concluded.

While I was happy that my suggestions worked, I was concerned that a second-year teacher would need that much direction. Certain aspects of teaching are instinctive, and one of those aspects is to be sure that your students behave when you take them outside of the classroom. Another is to never turn your back on students unless you are writing something on the board in the midst of an engaging lesson. Another is to move through the building with your classes, not follow behind by several minutes.

This case study reinforces the idea that there is no substitute for planning thoroughly and no substitute for anticipating challenges to the learning process. Young teachers who lack instinctive skills must compensate by planning thoroughly for each deviation in the regular classroom routine.